**VOLUME I
MANUAL**

GIRLS WITH SWORDS

Strategies For Winning Against The Enemies of Purpose

PASTOR TAUNDRA D. WILLIAMS
(THE DESTINY MIDWIFE)
DR. MICHELLE ROUCHE   PASTOR LAURA TORRES
PROPHET APRYL ESSIEN   CAROL HARDY
BONUS CHAPTER - PASTOR LEE A. WILLIAMS III

Copyright © 2024 by Destiny Speaks International, LLC

All Rights Reserved. Printed in the United States of America

All scripture quotations, unless otherwise indicated, are taken from the New King James Version®. Copyright © 1982 by Thomas Nelson, Inc. Used by permission.

All rights reserved. Scripture quotations marked —KJV are taken from the King James Version of the Holy Bible. Scripture quotations marked —NIV are taken from the Holy Bible, New International Version®. Copyright © 1973, 1978, 1984 by International Bible Society. Used by permission of Zondervan Publishing House. All rights reserved. Scripture quotations marked —NASB are taken from the New American Standard Bible. Copyright © 1960, 1962, 1963, 1968, 1971, 1972, 1973, 1975, 1977, 1995 by The Lockman Foundation.

The emphasis within scripture quotations are the author's own. This book is protected by the copyright laws of the United States of America. No part of this publication may be reproduced, distributed, or transmitted in any form or by any means, including photocopying, recording, or other electronic or mechanical methods, without the prior written permission of the publisher, except in the case of brief quotations embodied in critical reviews and certain other noncommercial uses and groups are permitted by copyright law and encouraged.

For permission requests, write to the publisher, addressed.

Attention: Permissions Coordinator, at this address destinyspeaksintl@gmail.com

Ordering Information: Quantity sales. Special discounts are available on quantity purchases by corporations, associations, and others. For details, contact the publisher at the email address above.

For more information, or to book an event, contact destinyspeaks.org

Book & Cover Design by Taundra D. Williams

ISBN 978-1-7349495-7-5

TESTIMONIES WANTED

Grace and Peace, Beloved *GIRLS WITH SWORDS!*

Your voice is vital, and the time has come to lift others from the shadows of despair into the light of freedom. Reflect on the powerful truth of Genesis 50:20 (NLT): "You intended to harm me, but God intended it all for good. He brought me to this position so I could save the lives of many people." This scripture has been a beacon in my journey, a reminder that what was meant to kill me is the very thing that pushes me.

Many of us have endured unimaginable trials. Your survival is proof that you possess a powerful testimony—one that can lift others from despair, break chains, and usher in a life of freedom in Christ.

Embrace this declaration with me: **"It's Bigger Than Me!"** Indeed, it transcends us all! Your trials have not only strengthened you but positioned you to offer hope and deliverance to others. Your story is not just your own—it's a lifeline, a clarion call of resilience and redemption.

If your heart cries out **"YES!"**, then I invite you to join forces with courageous women worldwide. We're on a mission to wield our voices like swords, shattering lies and freeing those still bound. This isn't just about sharing testimonies—it's a transformative journey from local events to global stages, awakening every silenced woman.

CALL TO ACTION

- Become A Girl With A Sword TODAY!
- Write, speak, and travel globally to share your story.
- Shine on virtual platforms and live stages in workshops, conferences, seminars, podcasts, and publications.
- Travel with us as we remove the muzzles off people from cities, states, and continents, sharing the Revival Fire once lost and now found again.

Believe it or not, there is a resurgence happening, and many of you are surviving on bated breath and need to be resuscitated. The world is waiting for your voice. When Destiny Speaks, how will you answer?

You're a chosen generation and royal priesthood touched by God, and He's ready to work through you to heal a nation.

Let's unite to unmuzzle the silence and become **THE UNMUTED EVERYWHERE!**

It's Time! Write, Speak, & Travel with the Destiny Midwife.

If this resonates with your calling, visit destinyspeaks.org to schedule an appointment to work with the Destiny Midwife. Decide today to unmute your voice with purpose, ignite hope for generations, and let your journey inspire nations.

After all, your identity depends on it! **Destiny and Purpose await your YES!**

TABLE OF CONTENTS

DEDICATION……………..…....…...….........…..I

INTRODUCTION……………....…....…......II

STRATEGY ONE: IT'S BIGGER THAN ME - **BY TAUNDRA D. WILLIAMS**……………………..….14

STRATEGY TWO: I'M A BOSS WHO BOWS TO THE KING - **BY DR. MICHELLE ROCHE**………..33

STRATEGY THREE: AIN'T NO TIME FOR COWARD SOLDIERS - **BY PASTOR LAURA E. TORRES**……………………………………….....56

STRATEGY FOUR: WONDER WOMEN PRAY - **BY TAUNDRA D. WILLIAMS**……………..……..88

STRATEGY FIVE: SHE BELIEVED SHE COULD, SO SHE DID- **BY PROPHET APRYL ESSIEN**…..106

STRATEGY SIX: NO MORE EXCUSES - **BY TAUNDRA D. WILLIAMS**………………………..129

STRATEGY SEVEN: IT'S ALL OR NOTHING! CAROL HARDY**……………………………...157

STRATEGY EIGHT: SHEROS & HEROS - PASTOR LEE A. WILLIAMS, III……………………………177

MEET "THE DESTINY MIDWIFE" TAUNDRA D. WILLIAMS……………………...206

MEET DR. MICHELLE ROUCHE.......................... 211

MEET PASTOR LAURA E. TORRES 214

MEET PROPHET APRYL ESSIEN......................... 216

MEET CAROL HARDY 218

MEET PASTOR LEE A. WILLIAMS, III.................220

DEDICATION

This entire manual is dedicated to the Wonder Women & Men I call *"Sheros & Heros"* of Purpose who have shaped my journey. You all are the reasons; I must go forward without hesitation and complete all God has assigned to my life.

First I honor my mother, Zelma J. Turner, for your wisdom, grace, tenacity, love and constant support to the vision. You have been my constant pusher since birth and I am so thankful God chose you to bring me into this world! - Thank you Mama!

To my daughters Chiffon & Miracle, embodiments of strength and purpose thank you for pushing me into greater, when I wanted to give up; To my granddaughters, Jurnee', Chyna and Purpose, for your boundless potential and call on your lives continues to push me to leave a legacy for you to continue until Christ calls us home; To my loving sisters Ashley, Brenda, Althea, Rashonda and Chanelle for your unwavering love and support in anything I do.

To my late grandmothers Ella Mae and Gloria Ann, for your enduring legacies, prayers, and commitment to Christ;

To my Sister-Preacher friends who contributed, for your invaluable insights, tenacity, and love for the mission of *"She Visions Worldwide"* despite warfare and life challenges.

To my husband, Pastor Lee A. Williams, III, for believing in me and giving me a platform to wield my sword and throw my voice like an arrow and pushing me consistently with your affirmations and words of encouragement;

To my father, Bishop C. L. Turner, for nurturing my spiritual journey & pushing me to cultivate a consistent prayer life; To my *"Destiny Speaks & She Visions Worldwide Team of Daughters,"* your collective vision commitment, dedication, strength, love for the *Destiny Speaks* mission, sustain me and push me further into purpose daily! May we continue to walk in our God-given purpose with power to *LIVE Full and Die EMPTY!*

– *Taundra D. Williams*

INTRODUCTION

Every woman carries an inherent power: a sacred sword to wield against life's trials. And too often, we do not recognize the strength within us or know how to effectively use it against the unseen forces that oppose our purpose. – *Taundra D. Williams*

"Girls With Swords" is your basic instruction manual for understanding your divine purpose. unleashing the warrior within to conquer anything standing in your way to fulfill your purpose.

Born from the renowned She Visions Worldwide Conference, this book features contributions from six powerful voices. Five battle-tested women, modern day Prophets who have intimately experienced both spiritual warfare and victorious breakthrough, share their wisdom alongside a bonus chapter – from a potent sermon transformed into a powerful chapter by Pastor Lee A. Williams, III.

At the heart of this literary journey is visionary founder Taundra D. Williams, the "Destiny Midwife." Her prophetic voice has sparked a global movement igniting women to rise up as Spirit-led "Wonder Women" and relentlessly pursue their God ordained callings. This volume continues that journey, evolving from simply harnessing your power to actively engaging the spiritual warfare required to manifest your purpose in its fullness.

Drawing directly from the armor of God in Ephesians 6:11-18, you'll learn to wield your sword of purpose with skillful precision against the unseen enemies opposing your destiny. Whether you're a dreamer, a doer, a fighter, or seeking to rekindle your belief in God's promises for your life - this book is your battle cry and strategic guide.

Throughout the pages of this book, you will find:

- Identification of the specific spiritual forces seeking to derail your purpose (self-doubt, fear, societal expectations)

- Revelation of the full spiritual weapons of warfare at your disposal (armor of God, faith-based strategies)
- Mindset cultivation as a victorious spiritual conqueror
- Scripture-based tactics to overcome self-doubt and societal barriers
- A framework for forging an actionable plan to boldly march forward in your calling.

If you crave deeper understanding of your unique, God-breathed purpose and the confidence to powerfully manifest it, this manual is for you. No more wavering, no more defeat - you were born for such a time as this. ***Wield your sword!***

STRATEGY ONE
IT'S BIGGER THAN ME

Author: Taundra D. Williams

Embracing A Divine Mandate

I was super excited when I first heard the title of what I was speaking at the She Visions Worldwide 2024 Conference. While meditating, I knew it reflected something profound about our calling as Wonder Women of God. This mandate, this divine calling on our lives, transcends our individual desires and daily tasks. It points to a greater purpose defined by God Himself.

But it wasn't until I got to the church Saturday morning for day two that God turned it all around! Whew! He said to talk about Mary and Martha. I was going to go a whole other way, but God had different plans. This shift in direction reminded me that our mandate is truly bigger than us – it's about aligning with God's will, even when it surprises us.

The Sista Disciples Of Bethany

To grasp the depth of this mandate, let's journey into the powerful biblical story of Mary and Martha. In the heart of the Gospels, we find these sisters of Bethany, each interacting with Jesus in ways that highlight contrasting aspects of discipleship. Their home was a place Jesus frequented, offering us a rare glimpse into His more personal moments away from public ministry.

Martha is often remembered for her service and hospitality, while Mary is celebrated for her attentive listening and devotion. This dichotomy presents a vital lesson in balancing the practical service of our faith with deep, personal engagement with Christ. Understanding their roles and responses to Jesus offers invaluable insights into the essence of true discipleship and the prioritization of our spiritual journey over worldly distractions.

Breaking Barriers: Mary's Revolutionary Act

In first-century Jewish culture, women were not typically disciples of rabbis. By sitting at Jesus' feet, Mary was assuming the posture of a disciple, a role traditionally reserved for men. Jesus' affirmation of her choice was radical for that time, challenging societal norms and elevating the spiritual equality of women.

This cultural context adds depth to our understanding of Mary's choice. It wasn't just a matter of listening versus serving; it was a bold declaration of her spiritual identity and worth in God's eyes. We might not face the same cultural barriers as modern women, but we can draw inspiration from Mary's courage to prioritize her relationship with Jesus above societal expectations.

The Better Part: Prioritizing Christ's Presence

Picture the scene in Luke 10:38-42 where Jesus is visiting their home. While Martha busies herself with hospitality tasks, Mary sits at Jesus' feet, listening intently to His teachings. Mary's choice speaks volumes about the essence of discipleship. It's a deliberate act of prioritizing relationship over responsibility, presence over productivity.

Mary's choice is countercultural and revolutionary in our culture, which often measures worth by output and success by busyness. It invites us to reconsider our priorities and challenges us to ask ourselves where we are seeking validation and fulfillment. Are we, like Martha, caught up in the endless cycle of doing? Or are we willing, like Mary, to choose the better part?

Let me ask you something: When was the last time you sat at Jesus' feet, figuratively speaking? When did you last push aside your to-do list, silence your phone, and just bask in His presence? It's not easy, is it? Our world screams for our attention, demanding productivity at every turn. But Mary's example challenges us to resist that pull and choose intimacy with Christ above all else.

Worship as Warfare: Aligning with God's Purpose

Choosing the better part, as Mary exemplified, is fundamentally an act of worship. This posture of worship doesn't just draw us closer to God; it aligns our will with His. In this alignment, we find the power to wield our swords—our gifts, talents, and callings—precisely guided by a heart fully surrendered to Him.

Therefore, worship becomes more than just singing songs on Sunday morning. It transforms into a powerful form of spiritual warfare, a declaration of our devotion and our primary strategy against the enemies of our purpose. When we worship, we're not just expressing our love for God; we're positioning ourselves in the spiritual realm, ready for battle.

I remember a time when I was traveling all over, singing in my quartet group, "The Melodious Voices of San Antonio." The pressure was intense, and I felt overwhelmed and at a crossroads in my life. I had sung my entire life. However, I knew God called me to preach the gospel, make disciples, and intercede for his people.

After months of trying, we finally finished ONE SONG! I remember listening to the song with my husband and the producer in the studio. Tears began to stream down my face. In that moment, I realized that God wanted more than my voice through singing. He wanted an obedient, pure posture from me! He wanted total surrender. As I sat there, tears streaming down my face, I felt God's gentle rebuke: 'Taundra, I desire your presence more than your performance.' That day changed everything for me. I learned that my effectiveness in ministry is directly proportional to the time I spend at Jesus' feet."

Let's not forget Mary's act of anointing Jesus' feet with costly perfume! This is a beautiful picture of extravagant worship, so costly money cannot buy it! John 12:3 (NKJV) tells us that the perfume was worth a year's wages. Can you imagine pouring out something so valuable? I could! But Mary understood that no material possession was too precious to give to Jesus.

This challenges us to consider: What are we willing to pour out for Jesus? What comfort, security, and ambition are we willing to lay at His feet? True devotion often comes at a cost—whether it's our time, our resources, or our pride. But as Mary shows us, when we give our all to Jesus, the fragrance of our worship fills not just the room but impacts eternity.

Jesus' Gentle Rebuke: Identifying the Essential

Let's dive deeper into Jesus' response to Martha in Luke 10:41-42 (NKJV): "Martha, Martha, you are worried and troubled about many things. But one thing is needed, and Mary has chosen that good part, which will not be taken away from her."

The Greek word for "worried" is "merimnaō," which implies being anxious or distracted. Jesus isn't criticizing Martha's service; he is, in fact, looking at her anxious state of mind. He's addressing the heart behind the action. The Bible tells us to be anxious for nothing.

Cross-referencing this with Matthew 6:33, we see a similar principle: "But seek first the kingdom of God and His righteousness, and all these things shall be added to you." Both passages emphasize prioritizing our relationship with God above all else. This "one thing" Jesus speaks of isn't a task to be completed but a posture of the heart. It's about being present with Him, learning from Him, and allowing His presence to transform us from the inside out.

Storms and Stillness

The story of Mary and Martha doesn't end in Luke's Gospel. In John's Gospel, we see a poignant scene where Mary anoints Jesus' feet with costly perfume. This act deepens our understanding of what it means to live a life of devotion to Christ.

Mary's actions are a testament to her profound love and gratitude towards Jesus. They reflect a relationship that has grown in depth and intimacy over time. This challenges us to consider how our own trials and triumphs have shaped our relationship with Christ. Have they drawn us closer to Him, or have we allowed them to create distance?

The story of Mary and Martha confronts the realities of life's challenges, from personal loss to the trials of faith, reminding us that Christ is both our refuge and our strength. Martha's bold confession of faith in John 11, amid the grief of her brother Lazarus's death, and Mary's extravagant act of worship both illustrate the transformative impact of encountering Jesus in the midst of life's storms.

These women teach us that our challenges are not just obstacles to overcome but opportunities to deepen our faith. When life gets tough, do we run to Jesus or away from Him? Mary and Martha show us the power of running towards Him, even in our pain and confusion.

The Harmony of Service and Devotion

Mary and Martha's choices offer invaluable insights into the balance required to fully embrace our identity as Wonder Women in Christ. They beckon us to find harmony between devotion and action, teaching us that effective service must spring from a place of spiritual nourishment and alignment with God's will.

This balance is not about choosing one over the other but understanding the rhythm and flow of when to sit at the feet of Jesus and when to rise and serve. No more Martha(ing) alone. We must learn to serve and receive at the same time. It's about recognizing the moments that call for deep, contemplative devotion and the moments that call for action.

Dare To Be Different

Within the sacred contours of their story, Mary and Martha teach us not only about devotion and service but also about the courage it takes to live out our unique callings. In a world that often dictates our worth by how much we do, Whew! Mary's choice to sit at Jesus' feet profoundly declares spiritual priorities over societal pressures.

Martha's journey, too, is a powerful narrative of discovery and reflection. It prompts us to examine our own lives for the distractions and anxieties that may lead us away from our true purpose! The courage Martha displays in her service and later her openness to Jesus' gentle correction provide a roadmap for navigating our own spiritual journeys.

Let me tell you, stepping into your calling takes guts. It might mean saying no to good things and saying yes to God's best. It might mean facing criticism or misunderstanding from others. But remember, your calling is not about you – it's about the One who called you. When we understand that our mandate is bigger than us, it gives us the courage to step out in faith, even when it's scary.

Our Sword - Our Weapon in Spiritual Warfare

As Wonder Women equipped with the full armor of God, our daily lives are a testament to the power of choosing the better part. Each piece of the armor not only protects us but also empowers us to fulfill our divine calling. The Sword of the Spirit, representing our active engagement with God's Word, is crucial. Wielding our sword for purpose means using Scripture as a defense against spiritual opposition and as a guide for living.

Ephesians 6:17 (NKJV) tells us to take "the sword of the Spirit, which is the word of God." This isn't just about memorizing verses, though that's important. It's about letting God's Word shape our thoughts, guide our decisions, and transform our lives. When we're faced with challenges or decisions, do we turn to the Word first? Do we let it cut through our confusion and illuminate our path?

I've found that the more I immerse myself in scripture, the more clearly I can discern God's voice in my daily life. It's like tuning an instrument—the more we align ourselves with God's Word, the more in tune we become with His will. After all, the Bible says he is the word!

When Sorrow Strikes

Mary and Martha's reactions to their brother's death offer profound insights into navigating seasons of grief. Their story teaches us that it's natural to experience a spectrum of emotions in grief and that it's crucial to approach God with honesty and faith. Grief observed through their eyes encourages us to engage with our pain directly, not as a season to be avoided with distractions or busyness, but as a period of profound spiritual engagement and growth.

We see Martha's bold faith when she declares to Jesus, "Even now I know that whatever You ask of God, God will give You" (John 11:22 NKJV). And we see Mary's raw honesty when she falls at Jesus' feet, saying, "Lord, if You had been here, my brother would not have died" (John 11:32 NKJV). Both approaches moved Jesus deeply.

In our own seasons of grief, we can learn from Mary and Martha. It's okay to be honest with God about our pain, to ask questions, and to hold onto hope even when circumstances seem hopeless. Our grief doesn't diminish our faith—it can actually deepen it if we allow ourselves to experience God's presence in our pain.

Drawing Near: Cultivating Closeness with God

Many women struggle with guilt when they take time for spiritual refreshment. Remember, self-care is not selfish when it's centered on Christ. If you're battling this guilt, try reframing your quiet time as an act of obedience rather than indulgence.

Another common challenge is consistency. To overcome this, try the 'habit stacking' technique: attach your devotional time to an existing habit, like having your morning coffee. Soon, spending time with God will become as natural and necessary as your daily caffeine fix.

Remember, Wonder Women, our intimacy with God isn't a luxury—it's our lifeline. It's the source of our strength, wisdom, and purpose. So, let's commit to overcoming whatever stands in the way of our "Mary moments" with Jesus.

Armed & Anointed, to Answer The Call

As we embrace our identity as Wonder Women, we commit to a life of worship, purpose, and action, ensuring that we are always ready to face the challenges and opportunities that lie ahead. Let us move forward with confidence, knowing that our mission is bigger than ourselves and armed with the strength and wisdom that come from God alone.

Remember, Girls with Swords; our mandate is not just about facing the enemies of our purpose but about overcoming them with faith, focus, and the unwavering conviction that our mission is indeed bigger than ourselves. Through a heart of worship and the strategic use of our spiritual armor, we are equipped to fulfill our divine mandate, knowing that it's always bigger than us.

So, let's choose the better part, like Mary did. Let's serve with passion like Martha did. Let's grieve with hope and worship with abandon. Let's identify and deal with the "little foxes" that threaten our spiritual growth. And let's be willing to pour out our most precious possessions at Jesus' feet.

Our mandate is clear: to live lives that reflect God's glory, impact our world for His kingdom, and do it all from a place of intimate connection with Jesus. It's not always easy, but it's always worth it. When we align our hearts with God's purpose, we discover that we're capable of far more than we ever imagined.

So, Wonder Women, are you ready? Are you ready to sit at His feet and rise to serve with purpose and power? Are you ready to wield your sword and wear your armor? Are you ready to let your life be a testament to the greatness of our God? Because that's what it means to embrace the mandate that's bigger than us. And that's the adventure God is inviting us into. Let's go!

STRATEGY TWO
I'M A BOSS, BUT I BOW TO THE KING

Author: Dr. Michelle Rouche

DEDICATION: This chapter is dedicated to woman trying to understand her place, position, and posture in the body of Christ. May you come into the knowledge of your "sonship" and the beauty of the Father's thoughts toward you. May you forever understand that you were designed to bring forth much fruit.

Introduction

Before we go any further; may I be honest right out the gate? This chapter title was thought provoking, presumptuous, and challenging. When given the task of delivering this message at the She Visions

Conference I secretly wished for another title. There were other great ones. Surely my messaging would align with the title, "It's ALL or nothing" or "No More Excuses". I quickly adjusted my thoughts, and I did what (I hope) every preacher does, I prayed and waited for Holy Spirit to give me the message He desired to share. I'm grateful that He spoke.

Understanding Your Role As A Boss

To truly understand what it means to be a boss under God's authority, let's delve into some important questions that can guide our self-reflection. When starting to pen this chapter of the book I asked myself a series of qualifying questions. What is a boss? Am I a boss? What does it mean to bow? Does being a boss come with scrutiny? Who made me a boss?

These questions opened up to discovery, self-reflection, and more questions. I began to realize that my line of questioning was simply my inner thoughts seeking to cause me to second-guess who I am. I have to immediately silence her. She can't be the loudest voice. Her influence cannot be greater than what God said about me before I was in my mother's womb.

I remember a specific instance when these thoughts were particularly loud. I was preparing for a major presentation at a women's conference, and I felt overwhelmed by doubt. The enemy's whispers grew louder: "Who do you think you are? You're not qualified to speak on this topic." But as I prayed, I felt God reminding me of my purpose and His calling on my life. It was in that moment of vulnerability that I felt a quiet assurance, and I moved forward with confidence. This experience taught me the importance of silencing those doubting voices and standing firm in my God-given identity.

If you're reading this chapter I need you to silence that voice too. I'm really being polite. Tell Sis to SHUT UP. Say this out loud: "I am a BOSS"! Say it again. Say it until you believe it.

Defining A Boss In God's Kingdom

For purposes of our discussion I need to provide us with a working understanding of how I define the term boss. Merriam Webster defines boss as a person who exercises control or authority. I define a BOSS as a woman who understands her divine assignment, operates in her God given authority with the grace to carry out the mission given by her boss while being acutely aware that she has been given a sword to wield. She is a woman of AND under authority.

I fully understand that some women have not yet come into the revelation of who they are. You may be reading this with a lingering question; "am I a boss?" Beloved, knowing who you are makes you aware of who you aren't. The enemy has a vested interest in you remaining in an identity crisis. If you don't know who you are you also don't know what you are entitled to possess.

Let me illustrate this with an analogy. I want you to imagine joining a gym. You arrive at the facility and the perky, energetic employee gives you a tour. He points out all the equipment and its features. He tells you about the different classes, gives you a tour of the sauna, the hydro bed, the spin class, the yoga room, and the lockers. You're excited at all the gym has to offer so you sign up immediately however you only use the treadmill when you visit.

Sadly, this is a picture of many believers. We confessed Jesus as Lord and stopped there. Many have never tapped into the John 10:10(b) life. You can't be a boss if you don't know what you have access to. God has given us **EVERYTHING** that pertains to life and godliness (2 Peter 2:3 NKJV). Read that again.

I remember God telling me, I chose to partner with women to bring my plan into the earth. Women are the access point into the earth. Anything God wants to accomplish in the earth He partners with a woman. All of God's dreams, plans and purposes are realized in the womb of a woman. WOW! That's sobering. *"That's BIG. If that's not BOSS I don't know what is!"*

The problem isn't that we don't believe God. We don't believe in ourselves. As long as we are ignorant to who we are the enemy will have the advantage.

Understanding The Enemy's Tactics

Ephesians 6:11 KJV instructs us to "Put on the whole armor of God, that ye may be able to stand against the wiles of the devil." Oftentimes we read scripture in haste and tend to miss the subtleties. The Apostle Paul gives us key strategy in this verse. The first thing we need to understand is that we're not fighting the devil. He was already defeated by Jesus. The only power the devil possesses is the power we give him. He uses the power of suggestion and misinformation. The Bible declares that he is the father of lies. If what you're seeing is in direct opposition to the Word of God then it is a LIE from the devil.

Let's rewind a bit. Paul uses an unfamiliar term. So what are wiles? In its most simplistic meaning, wiles are tricks and deceptions. Wiles of the devil are those clever schemes used by Satan to ensnare us. **BUT THERE IS ANOTHER LEVEL**—let's go deeper.

In psychology and cognitive science, a schema (PLURAL: schemata or schemas) describes a pattern of thought or behavior that organizes categories of information and the relationships among them. It can also be described as a mental structure of preconceived ideas. Schemata influence attention and the absorption of new knowledge: people are more likely to notice things that fit into their schema, while re-interpreting contradictions to the schema as exceptions or distorting them to fit. Schemata tend to remain unchanged, even in the face of contradictory information. In other words, what we hold fast to will hold fast to us EVEN IF it is contrary to the Word of God.

To illustrate this concept, let's consider a practical example. Imagine a woman who has grown up believing she's not smart enough to succeed in her career. This belief becomes her schema. Even when she achieves great things at work, she might attribute her success to luck or downplay her accomplishments. Her schema fights against the reality of her capabilities. Understanding these concepts of wiles and schemata is crucial for recognizing and combating the enemy's strategies in our own lives. In our everyday experiences, we might face negative thoughts or lies about our worth and capabilities. By understanding that these are the enemy's wiles, we can reject these lies and replace them with God's truth about us. This shift in mindset is crucial for living out our divine authority.

We can receive a prophetic word, but that word has to make its way through our schema. Remember the gym example? We can have a plethora of amenities but still be tied to the only machine we know how to use. Your schema fights against your faith.

Recognizing The Enemy's Deceptions

BELOVED you have to understand that devil wages war to KEEP YOU tied to your **SCHEMATA.** We live in a culture that relies on horoscopes, sage, chakras, mediums, third eyes and **COUNTERFEITs** to the Holy Spirit. The devil is **STILL** using that same line he used on Eve…you shall not surely die. If you fornicate. If you lie… you shall not surely die. If you gossip… you shall not surely die. If you watch a little porn… you shall not surely die. If you don't wanna be married any more you can get another spouse…you shall not surely die. You don't really have to pray you can just journal and manifest everything…you shall not surely die. The devil really doesn't have any new tricks. His old ones are still working.

There was a popular song released in 2005 by Chamillionaire called Ridin' Dirty. The artist told the story of how the police were trying to catch him slipp'in. The enemy wants to catch you slipp'in. Paul tells us to dress for the occasion. We are commanded to put on the whole armor of God. Why? So that we can STAND. We are not wrestling against flesh and blood (Ephesians 6:12 NKJV). Our fight is spiritual.

Fighting is not optional. There are no non-combat positions in the Kingdom of God.

Since we are commissioned to this fight we have to understand our opponent. We have to understand his combat tactics so that we can counter them. Paul brings us into the War Room to lay out the plan. The war room was first introduced, obviously, during war times. It was where military leaders and generals discussed their tactics and strategies. The Bible is our book of strategies. You can't **BOSS UP without instructions from the BOSS.**

The Power Within Us

I feel compelled to share a fundamental truth with you in an effort to establish your God given authority in this earth realm. Romans 8:11 **NLT** gives us a front row seat into what believers possess. "The Spirit of God, who raised Jesus from the dead, lives in you.

"READ THAT AGAIN! Wait, what? Is the Apostle Paul really saying the exact same spirit God used when He raised Jesus is on the inside of me? **YES!** A thousand times **YES.** Beloved, you don't have a measure, you don't have a diluted version, you don't have generic great value brand spirit; you have the very same spirit living and moving on the inside of you. This truth is almost too wonderful to fathom. The Creator of everything has made this kind of power available to you and me. There is no devil in hell that can defeat you with this kind of power.

Let's pause for a moment and really let this sink in. Imagine the power it took to raise Jesus from the dead. That same power - not a fraction, not a diluted version - but that exact same power resides in you. How does this change the way you view your challenges? Your purpose? Your potential? This is not just theological rhetoric; this is a game-changing reality that should transform how we live our daily lives.

The weapons will form but they won't prosper. We are afflicted in every way, but not crushed; perplexed, but not driven to despair; persecuted, but not forsaken; struck down, but not destroyed; always carrying in the body the death of Jesus, so that the life of Jesus may also be manifested in our bodies. (2 Corinthians 4:8-10 ESV) Real talk; "Life be Life'n"

BUT —God be God'n!' I love that so much I made a T-shirt for purchase.

Understanding God's Cheat Codes

The Bible literally gives us cheat codes. (1 Peter 4:12-13 KJV) says "Beloved, think it not strange concerning the fiery trial which is to try you, as though some strange thing happened unto you: But rejoice, inasmuch as ye are partakers of Christ's sufferings; that, when his glory shall be revealed, ye may be glad also with exceeding joy." Indulge me if you will. Here's the MRV (Michelle's revealed version) Sis, don't be surprised or get caught slippin' when life starts line'n. Don't trip. God's got you. This pressure will not break you. It's all a part of the God's plan to show out on your behalf. Relax, turn on your favorite praise song and dance because ′El Shaddai is doing His thing.

He is ′El Shaddai, Almighty God. He also has military prowess as the LORD of Hosts/Armies (Yahweh-Sabaoth). "Almighty God" (′El-Shaddai) is the title by which God reveals himself to Abraham. The term appears as "′El Shaddai" (Almighty God) seven times, and standing alone as "Shaddai" (The Almighty) 41 times in the Old Testament and 9 times in the New Testament (as Greek pantokratōr; 2

Corinthians 6:18; Revelation 1:8; 4:8; 11:17; 15:3; 16:7, 14; 19:15; and 21:22). Abraham knew God as a Mighty Warrior. I have a question for you. How can you lose with this kind of backing? Sis, you're not just a girl with a sword, you are a girl with an army.

Understanding Our Role

The first thing we must understand about an army/group is that every effective organized body has a leader, followers, a mission, a strategy, core values and written SOP. An **SOP is a standard operating procedure.** A standard operating procedure is a set of written instructions that describes the step-by-step process that must be taken to properly perform a routine activity. SOPs should be followed the exact same way every time to guarantee that the organization remains consistent. An effective standard operating procedure clearly explains the steps taken to complete a task and informs the employee (believers/soldiers) of any risks associated with the process.

Remember 1 Peter 4:12-13? Here are a few more **"occupational hazards"** for soldiers:

- **2 Timothy 2:3-6 KJV** "Thou therefore endure hardness, as a good soldier of Jesus Christ. No man that warreth entangleth himself with the affairs of this life; that he may please him who hath chosen him to be a soldier."
- **Romans 8:36 KJV** "As it is written, For thy sake we are killed all the day long; we are accounted as sheep for the slaughter."
- **Romans 8:18 KJV** "For I reckon that the sufferings of this present time are not worthy to be compared with the glory which shall be revealed in us."

- **2 Timothy 3:12 NIV** "In fact, everyone who wants to live a godly life in Christ Jesus will be persecuted."
- **Matthew 5:10–12 ESV** "Blessed are those who are persecuted for righteousness' sake, for theirs is the kingdom of heaven. Blessed are you when others revile you and persecute you and utter all kinds of evil against you falsely on my account. Rejoice and be glad, for your reward is great in heaven, for so they persecuted the prophets who were before you."
- **James 1:12 NIV** "Blessed is the one who perseveres under trial because, having stood the test, that person will receive the crown of life that the Lord has promised to those who love him."
- **Romans 5:3-5 NIV** "Not only so, but we also glory in our sufferings, because we know that suffering produces perseverance;

perseverance, character; and character, hope. And hope does not put us to shame, because God's love has been poured out into our hearts through the Holy Spirit, who has been given to us."

- **James 1:2-4 NIV** "Consider it pure joy, my brothers and sisters, whenever you face trials of many kinds, because you know that the testing of your faith produces perseverance. Let perseverance finish its work so that you may be mature and complete, not lacking anything."

The Importance Of Following God's Word

The Holy Bible is our SOP. I want to reiterate a portion of the definition; "should be followed the exact same way". That bears repeating. Can we rewind it all the way back to Genesis 3:1-5 ASV? "Now the serpent was more subtle than any beast of the field which Jehovah God had made. And he said unto the woman, Yea, hath God said, Ye shall not eat of any tree of the garden? And the woman said unto the serpent, Of the fruit of the trees of the garden we may eat: but of the fruit of the tree which is in the midst of the garden, God hath said, Ye shall not eat of it, neither shall ye touch it, lest ye die. And the serpent said unto the woman, Ye shall not surely die: for God doth know that in the day ye eat thereof, then your eyes shall be opened, and ye shall be as God, knowing good and evil."

The Danger Of Adding To God's Word

In Genesis 3:3, Eve attempts to recite or repeat what God said in Genesis 2:16-17 NIV: "And the Lord God commanded the man, "You are free to eat from any tree in the garden; but you must not eat from the tree of the knowledge of good and evil, for when you eat from it you will certainly die."" There is a slight difference in what Eve said and what God said. Eve added a little "razzle dazzle" to what she told the enemy. When the enemy realized she was fluent in "razzle dazzle" he added his own.

Beloved we have to be careful that we are doing the Word of God "the exact same way" he told us because when we don't it opens the door to the death cycle. The enemy lies because that's all he knows how to do. He is the father of lies. He told Eve you shall not surely die. LIES! Surely still means SURELY. We can't get mad at the results we don't get because we didn't do what God said like He said it.

Let's apply this principle to our daily lives. How often do we add our own interpretation to God's Word? Maybe we rationalize certain behaviors or make exceptions for ourselves. But just like Eve, when we deviate from God's exact instructions, we open ourselves up to the enemy's deception. It's crucial that we study and apply God's Word accurately, without adding our own **"razzle dazzle"**.

The Consequences Of Sin

Bowing to the King means that His established order is what I follow. **Proverbs 14:12 NIV "There is a way that appears to be right, but in the end it leads to death."** You shall surely die. Let's gain clarity on what surely die means. In Christian theology, spiritual death is separation from God caused by sin. **"Your sins have separated you and God" (Isaiah 59:2 NIV).** When you SIN- i.e., miss the mark, disobey God the Bible tells us that the wages of sin is death. Not probation, not house arrest, not community service. There is only one punishment—**DEATH.**

This might seem harsh at first glance, but it's crucial to understand the gravity of sin and its consequences. Sin isn't just about breaking rules; it's about breaking relationship with our Creator. It's a rejection of His love and authority in our lives. When we truly grasp this, we begin to see why God takes sin so seriously.

God's Solution For Sin

God knew that there was no alternative to your punishment. He did not want your punishment to be death so he sent Jesus through a woman to die for you. He knew no sin but He died in your place. He died in my place. I'm in awe of His love towards me. I am rendered speechless at His grand gesture. I am who I am because of Jesus. I'm a Boss who bows to the King.

Let's take a moment to reflect on this incredible truth. The God of the universe loved us so much that He was willing to take on human form and die in our place. This isn't just religious rhetoric; it's a life-changing reality. When we truly understand

and embrace this love, it transforms how we see ourselves and how we live our lives.

Living As A Boss Who Bows To The King

As bosses who bow to the King, we operate from a place of incredible privilege and responsibility. We have been given authority, but we use it under the ultimate authority of God. This balance of power and submission is what sets us apart as Christian leaders.

Consider how this plays out in your daily life. **How does knowing you're a *"Boss who bows to the King"* affect your decision-making? Your interactions with others? Your approach to challenges?**

It's not about throwing our weight around or demanding respect. Instead, it's about humbly and confidently walking in the authority God has given us, always remembering that we answer to a higher power.

STRATEGY THREE

AIN'T NO TIME FOR COWARD SOLDIERS

Author: Pastor Laura E. Torres

DEDICATION: To My husband, Pastor Ray Torres, My partner of 32 years. Founder of Sold-Out Believers Church now known as New Direction Church San Antonio. Thank you for your love and for always pushing me to be the woman of God that He has purposed for me to be. You have consistently looked beyond my flaws and have always inspired me to continue to be resilient, brave, and gritty.

To my sons, son in law and grandsons each of you have inspired me to continue to run the race with perseverance and purpose. To my two daughters, daughters in love, my granddaughters, sisters and sister-in-laws, nieces, and daughters in the faith. I am honored to be part of your life. I am dedicated to living my life alongside of you knowing that we are girls with swords and we have been called to be women —of purpose on purpose for a purpose. No matter the circumstances or difficult situations we face we must face it with bravery, resilience, tenacity, and strategy. Now Girls, —Swing your swords.

Introduction: The Call to Courage

Luke 9:62 (NIV) states, "No one who puts his hand to the plow and looks back is fit for the kingdom." The Message translation puts it this way: "Jesus said, 'No procrastination. No backward look. You can't put God's kingdom off till tomorrow. Seize the day.'"

Can you recall a time in your life when you felt like you were on fire for the Lord? Have you ever felt as though you were riding on a cloud, filled with an unshakeable belief that the Lord has called you to accomplish great and mighty deeds in His name? But then, without warning, something disrupts your peace, casting you into a state of perplexity and doubt. In those moments, feelings of inadequacy creep in, and you begin to question whether the Lord might have chosen the wrong person for the task. You find yourself thinking, "Surely, the Lord meant to call someone else, not me."

Perhaps you've experienced this internal struggle recently. You might even shake your head, saying, "No, I'm not afraid!" But the truth is, we all have times when we feel unsure and scared on our journey of faith. Have you felt cowardly lately?

You may be reading this and saying, "Who me, a coward? Absolutely not! I ain't no coward! "Well, let's dive deeper into what being a coward really means in the context of our spiritual journey.

What is A Coward In The Spiritual Realm?

By definition, the word coward is: a person who lacks the courage to do or endure dangerous or unpleasant things, one who shows disgraceful fear or timidity. In other words, a coward is someone who is a quitter, a weakling, a sneak, a pushover, a sissified Christian, or a sissy lala, someone who puts their hands to the plow and looks back. A person who is not brave and is too eager to avoid danger, someone who tends to avoid difficulty or pain.

Examples Of A Coward

Someone who has deserted his troops; A soldier who ran as soon as the first shots were fired; A person who runs away from war and retreats back to his or her present state of being.

In our spiritual walk, cowardice might manifest as shrinking back from God's calling, refusing to step out in faith, or being paralyzed by fear when faced with challenges. It's crucial to recognize these tendencies in ourselves so we can address them head on.

Life's Curveballs

Sometimes life can throw us curve balls, grenades, spit wads, uppercuts, low blows, and some are blows to our liver in the boxing ring, which knock us out. Perhaps, it is just a small "Boo" and we get blown off our chair. It can also be a small hiccup, and we get perturbed. Perhaps we forget that in every battle we face, we will have battle scars and our Armor will get scuffed, dented, and banged up. These challenges are not meant to defeat us but to refine us. They are opportunities for growth, for deepening our faith, and for showcasing God's strength in our weakness. As we navigate these difficult moments, it's essential to remember that our identity is not in our performance but in Christ.

Embracing Bravery

What is the opposite of a Coward? Or being cowardly? A brave one, someone who is brave, a warrior, a soldier, a powerhouse, a solid man, courageous, a battler, a fighter, a lion, a lioness, a hero, someone who is not easily moved by the winds or storms in life.

2 Corinthians 4:8-9 (NLT) says, "We are pressed on every side by troubles, but we are not crushed. We are perplexed, but not driven to despair. We are hunted down but never abandoned by God. We get knocked down, but we are not destroyed." This scripture reminds us that even in our toughest moments, God is with us. It's not about never facing difficulties, but about how we face them - with courage, resilience, and faith in God's unfailing presence and power.

The Inner Battle: Confidence vs. Insecurity

Many times, we find ourselves not feeling confident or courageous due to various reasons. While we may appear brave on the outside, the reality is that there are moments when we feel quite the opposite.

At times, we may present a brave and composed exterior, appearing confident and capable. We look the part, we dress the part, yet, inwardly, we may be torn, broken, misunderstood, perplexed, or feeling inadequate and timid. Sometimes our insecurities scream louder than our Faith.

A Personal Journey Through Struggle

There was a time in my life when I faced a situation that demanded surrendering to the Lord. It plunged me into agony, making me feel as though my world had all crumbled. I questioned my calling and felt like I had emptied every single fruit from my basket. Overwhelmed with emptiness, disgrace, perplexity, and shame, I yielded to cowardice, on the brink of giving up entirely. My emotions raced at breakneck speed, and I felt exposed, as if everyone could see the turmoil within me.

Let me share a specific instance. During this period, I was faced with the challenge of leading a major project at my church. Despite my initial enthusiasm, doubts began to creep in as the deadline approached. I remember one night, sitting alone in my living room, surrounded by unfinished plans and a growing sense of inadequacy. I thought about all the people relying on me and felt paralyzed by the fear of letting them down.

The pressure was immense. Each morning, I forced myself to smile and encourage others, but inside, I was battling a storm. My prayers seemed to go unanswered, and I questioned if I was truly the right person for the job. One day, after a particularly discouraging meeting, I broke down in tears. I cried out to God, asking why He had placed me in this position if I wasn't capable of fulfilling it.

It was in that moment of vulnerability that I felt a quiet assurance. I remembered the story of Gideon and how he, too, felt inadequate yet was called a mighty warrior by God. This realization didn't immediately solve my problems, but it gave me the strength to keep going. I started to see my challenges as opportunities for growth rather than insurmountable obstacles.

The Refining Power of Struggle

I believe that moments of struggle and adversity have the power to shape us into stronger individuals with a deeper understanding of ourselves and our faith. It's often through facing challenges and overcoming obstacles that we develop resilience, courage, and a stronger reliance on God's strength. These experiences can refine our character, deepen our faith, and ultimately equip us to fulfill the purpose and calling that God has for our lives.

Genesis 50:20 (NIV) says, "You intended to harm me, but God intended it for good to accomplish what is now being done, the saving of many lives." This verse reminds us that even in our most difficult moments, God is working for our good and for His greater purpose. What seems like a setback or failure to us might be the very thing God uses to prepare us for a greater mission.

Biblical Examples of Courage and Struggle

The Bible contains numerous stories of courageous men and women who have exhibited strength, bravery, and determination in various forms of conflict and adversity. From Deborah, the Prophet and judge who led Israel into battle against their enemies, to Esther, who risked her life to save her people from destruction, these women demonstrated remarkable resilience and faith in the face of danger. Their stories serve as powerful examples of how women have played vital roles in the battles for justice, freedom, and righteousness throughout history.

However, there are also numerous stories of men and women who struggled with doubts and feelings of inadequacy. These are common experiences, even among those who are chosen by God for special purposes. However, God's grace, strength, and guidance enable them to overcome their insecurities and fulfill their calling in His plan.

Embracing Your Divine Calling

It is vital for us to understand that we will all go through times in our lives when mixed emotions will try to deviate us from accomplishing all that the Lord has called us to do. Oh, but my sister, as you are reading this chapter, I pray that you are reminded that you must know that you know, that you know that you know, that the Lord has called you and has made no mistake in calling you to accomplish the task He has called you to do. No one else is called to fulfill your destiny. There is only one of you, and The Lord has called you.

Gideon: A Warrior Wrestling with Inadequacy

There is a story in the Bible that I would like to share with you of a particular man who was a warrior, but he was a Warrior who wrestled with hesitation and inadequacy.

Have you struggled with hesitation or inadequacy? Perhaps, you felt like a hesitant or inadequate soldier! By definition, the word hesitant is the state of being unsure, uncertain, doubtful, tentative, or undecided.

Gideon initially doubted his own abilities and questioned whether he was the right person to lead Israel in the battle against the Midianites.

The Lord sent an angel to appear to him and called him "Mighty Warrior". Although at that moment Gideon did not feel like a warrior, much less a Mighty Warrior. Gideon expressed his disbelief by pointing out his family's insignificance and his own lack of strength. Gideon was seeking assurance through multiple signs from God, such as the fleece test. It took Gideon a while before he accepted his role as a leader and warrior. His hesitation stemmed from feelings of inadequacy and uncertainty about his capacity to fulfill the task God had given him.

Gideon's Story:

A Reflection of Our Own Struggles

Gideon's story is a powerful reminder for us today. Just as Gideon doubted his own abilities, many of us often feel inadequate when faced with daunting tasks or challenges in our own lives. We might think, "Who am I to do this?" or "I don't have what it takes." However, God's choice of Gideon shows us that He sees potential in us that we often cannot see in ourselves. When we are called to step into roles that seem overwhelming, we can take comfort in knowing that God equips those He calls.

In Judges 6, we see a story where the Israelites had done evil in the sight of the Lord, and so He gave them into the hand of the Midianites. The Israelites became very afraid of the evil and oppressive Midianites; for 7 years, they ravaged through their land, destroyed their homes, their crops, and killed their families. Gideon and the Israelites were afraid and scared for their lives.

One thing that is interesting about Gideon is that there were times when he was very courageous and showed bravery, but there were also times when he would waver and retreat. There were both moments where he had a loss of courage and moments where he held back. Have there been moments like this you have faced?

We see His bravery and his courage in the fact that he was the only family member that worshipped the True God. All the other family members worshipped the other god Baal. The ridicule and persecution he had to face sounds all too familiar to many of us.

Gideon also faced times of fear. He was unsure if he had the attributes to be able to defend his family from the cruel Midianites. He was simultaneously courageous and full of fear.

The Angel's Message: You Are a Mighty Warrior

In Judges 6:11, we see an Angel of the Lord appear to Gideon while he was threshing wheat in the winepress. The Angel declared, "The Lord is with you, Mighty Warrior!"

He was threshing wheat in a winepress because he was scared to death that the Midianites were going to come and steal his harvest. So, the idea that he was a mighty warrior just didn't make any sense... Surely, nobody would have looked at Gideon and called him a mighty warrior.

I am here to tell you today that whether you feel like the Lord is with you or not, He is with you! The Lord sees more in us than we see in ourselves.

Four Points for Facing Uncertainty

Here are four points that you can utilize as practical guidance when facing uncertainty and resisting the urge to retreat.

1. Every Warrior Must Fight the Inner Fear of Failure: Judges 6:14 (NIV) says, "The Lord turned to him and said, 'Go in the strength you have and save Israel out of Midian's hand. Am I not sending you?"

The Lord was saying you have a battle to fight, a battle to win, a kingdom to advance. I have prepared you, you are equipped, and you are a Mighty Warrior. This is your kingdom assignment. Remember that the Lord does not call the equipped; He equips the called!

Gideon brings out his resume... "My clan is the weakest; I am the least of my family." What he was saying was, "But Lord, I am not good enough." He was bringing out all the reasons why he thought God should choose someone else. His reasoning for God to seek a better candidate than him was a long list.

Fear of failure is a common challenge that many warriors, leaders, and individuals often face. It's a natural human emotion that can arise when confronted with challenges, uncertainties, or high stakes situations. Learning to face our fears is not just a crucial step; it becomes the epitome of personal growth, resilience, and ultimately, achieving success. When we confront our fears head-on, we not only expand our comfort zones but also discover the depths of our inner strength and courage. Each challenge overcome becomes a steppingstone, propelling us forward on the path to realizing our full potential. In embracing our fears, we unlock new opportunities for growth, resilience, and ultimately, triumph.

Warriors throughout history, whether in battle or in personal struggles, have had to confront their inner fears of failure. They must cultivate courage, determination, and confidence to press forward despite the risks and uncertainties. Acknowledging and accepting the possibility of failure is the first step toward overcoming it. By embracing a growth mindset and viewing failures as learning opportunities rather than setbacks, warriors can turn their fears into sources of strength and resilience.

Proverbs 15:22 (NIV) says, "Without counsel plans fail, but with many advisers they succeed."

In our pursuit of purpose, it is essential to be surrounded by spiritual mentors, allies, and spiritual guidance. This provides valuable encouragement and a better perspective during times of fear and doubt. Ultimately, facing and conquering the inner fear of failure builds character, courage, and the capacity for enduring success.

Have you felt the Lord prompting you to do something, or perhaps He is leading you to do something, and you say... BUT LORD, I cannot? How many times have you begun to pull out a list of why we cannot and why we should not?! HELLO??!!

Ouch and Amen!!

2. Get Out of the Winepress! God was telling Gideon to "Get out of the Winepress." The fact that Gideon was threshing wheat in a winepress was significant. Wheat was normally threshed on threshing floors. Threshing floors were hard, smooth open spaces prepared on either rock or clay and carefully chosen for maximum exposure to the prevailing winds. This was done so that the winds would blow the straw away, as the grain was tossed into the wind together with the straw, leaving the actual grain to fall on the floor. Threshing floors were visible spaces and definitely not a place to hide.

Winepresses were the opposite. They were square or circular pits which were either made out of rocks or dug out of the ground. Gideon threshed out his wheat underground in a winepress, not in an exposed threshing floor. Why underground? So that he could hide from the prying eyes of his enemies --

the Midianites, who were ready to confiscate whatever little grain he was threshing.

Let's look into Gideon's winepress here for a moment: His mindset was gloomy and depressed. He had lost hope of any redemption out of his situation. He had lost faith in the God who redeemed his ancestors from Egypt. He felt rejected by God. But God had a plan for his life. God wanted him out of the winepress and onto the battlefield to do exploits for God's glory.

The Winepress Mentality: A Modern Perspective

Just like Gideon, we often find ourselves hiding in our own "winepresses," avoiding the challenges we are meant to face. For example, you might be avoiding a difficult conversation with a loved one, fearing the potential conflict. Instead of addressing the issue head-on, you might bury yourself in work or other distractions, hoping the problem will resolve itself. However, just as Gideon had to step out of his hiding place to fulfill his calling, we too must confront our fears and take action.

Another example is in the workplace. Imagine you have an innovative idea that could significantly improve your team's efficiency, but you're afraid to speak up because you worry about rejection or criticism. Staying silent is akin to hiding in the winepress. To grow and make an impact, you need to step out in faith, share your idea, and trust that God will guide you through any challenges that arise. I know that there have been numerous times in my life that I felt inadequate, underqualified, hesitant, doubtful of God calling me to fulfill the call of God upon my life. It was easier to stay home, stay in a dark place, or stay away in my winepress which was hidden and looking busy so that I didn't have to be on the threshing floor where others could see me.

You might find yourself in a winepress today, thinking all is lost. The winepress comes with a sense of failure, inadequacy, and hopelessness. It comes with a feeling of divine rejection. But the winepress is not your assigned final destination. God wants you out of the winepress and onto the battlefield to do some exploits. So, let us incline our ears carefully to the voice of the angel of the Lord and come out of the winepress today! God sees you as a mighty warrior ready to come out and do exploits in His Name!

3. *The Way Forward Sometimes Starts By Taking Two Steps Back:* Judges 7:1-3 (NLT) says, "So Jerub-baal (that is, Gideon) and his army got up early and went as far as the spring of Harod. The armies of Midian were camped north of them in the valley near the hill of Moreh. The Lord said to Gideon, 'You have too many warriors with you. If I let all of you fight the Midianites, the Israelites will boast to me that they saved themselves by their own strength. Therefore, tell the people, 'Whoever is timid or afraid may leave this mountain and go home."' So 22,000 of them went home, leaving only 10,000 who were willing to fight."

Gideon started off with 32,000 soldiers. After the announcement, 22,000 cowards went home and 10,000 soldiers remained. The army was still too massive. So another sweep of potential spectators was necessary. The remaining 10,000 were asked to go down to the spring.

Judges 7:4-7 (NLT) continues, "But the Lord told Gideon, 'There are still too many! Bring them down to the spring, and I will test them to determine who will go with you and who will not.' When Gideon took his warriors down to the water, the Lord told him, 'Divide the men into two groups. In one group put all those who cup water in their hands and lap it up with their tongues like dogs. In the other group put all those who kneel down and drink with their mouths in the stream.' Only 300 of the men drank from their hands. All the others got down on their knees and drank with their mouths in the stream. The Lord told Gideon, 'With these 300 men I will rescue you and give you victory over the Midianites. Send all the others home.'"

After this simple exercise, only 300 would be chosen to go to war. Only 300 soldiers out of 32,000 who originally showed up were qualified. This simple exercise separated the Gladiators from the Spectators. There were 31,700 cowards that showed up to go to battle. I'm almost sure they also struggled with inadequacy, inferiority, doubt, and excuses. These individuals might have also carried around a resume showing why they could not go to war.

Gideon was uncertain about going to war with 32,000 soldiers and now he was only left with 300. His knees might have been shaking by now, his hands are probably sweaty and clammy. Most times it looks like the battle has already been lost without even starting the battle. The way forward will sometimes require us to take two steps back. We have to learn to trust the process.

Philippians 1:6 (NIV) says, "Being confident of this, that he who began a good work in you will carry it on to completion until the day of Christ Jesus."

The Power of Standing Firm

These 300 brave men would be the ones that displayed keeping their eyes on the cross, swinging their swords and lapping water with the opposite hand. I can close my eyes and picture them doing their warrior dance while swinging their swords against the enemy. **In Judges 7:21 the Bible says,** "While each man held his position." The advancement took place when they took their stand and when they took their ground. Your greatest victories and your greatest fears go hand in hand!

4. Don't Look Back! Luke 9:62 (Message) says, "Jesus said, 'No procrastination. No backward looks. You can't put God's kingdom off till tomorrow. Seize the day.'"

The meaning of "putting your hands to the plow" implies to begin or to undertake a task. The moment we make a commitment, or we engage in a task the Lord sets before us, we will have thoughts of looking back. It is important to understand that... There is nothing back there that you left behind that you still need to go get!

The Danger of Looking Back

Genesis 19:17 (NIV) says, "As soon as they had brought them out, one of them said, 'Flee for your lives! Don't look back, and don't stop anywhere in the plain! Flee to the mountains or you will be swept away!'"

Look at Lot's wife. She looked back and immediately turned into a pillar of salt. She looked back with a degree of longing to return to what she had left behind. She had a yearning for the lifestyle she lived in Sodom and Gomorrah. The distraction of her past was present in her life. The Hebrew word for "looked back" means more than to glance over one's shoulder. It means "to regard, to consider or to pay attention to." Despite the warning from the angels to flee without looking back, her heart was still attached to the sinful lifestyle and material comforts of her past. As a result, she disobeyed the command and looked back, facing the consequences of her disobedience.

Choosing to follow God's will in our lives will force us out of our comfort zone. Most of us in ministry have had to make sacrifices that we are not accustomed to, and this is something Lot's wife struggled to endure. Her heart wasn't ready to fully surrender. She didn't know who she was, much less know who her God was. She quit before she even got started.

At times, we may desire to follow God's will, yet find that our hearts are not fully prepared to surrender, and we are hesitant to embrace change. Struggling with constantly looking back can be a challenging pattern to break.

Let me remind you that there are no rearview mirrors in serving Christ. There is nothing back there that we need to go get.

Embracing Our Call as Courageous Warriors

In conclusion, the journey of faith often presents us with moments of uncertainty, doubt, and fear. We may find ourselves hesitating, feeling inadequate, or even tempted to retreat. However, as we've explored through the stories of Lot's wife and Gideon, as well as the teachings of Scripture, God calls us to be courageous warriors who are "Girls with Swords", trusting His guidance and provision.

We are reminded that fear of failure, hiding in our "winepresses," and looking back at our past can hinder us from fully embracing God's calling on our lives. But through faith and obedience, we can overcome these obstacles and step into the fullness of what God has prepared for us.

Key Takeaways

Face Your Fears: Just as Gideon overcame his doubts and fears, we too can conquer our insecurities by trusting in God's strength and guidance.

Step Out of Your Winepress: Like Gideon, we need to step out of our hiding places and confront the challenges before us.

Don't Look Back: The story of Lot's wife teaches us the dangers of longing for the past. To fully embrace God's calling, we must focus on the present and future.

Embrace God's Vision of You: Remember, God sees us as mighty warriors even when we don't see it in ourselves.

Trust the Process: Sometimes, the way forward involves taking steps that don't make sense to us, but we must trust God's plan.

As we face the challenges and uncertainties of life, let us remember the words of Jesus: *"No procrastination. No backward looks. You can't put God's kingdom off till tomorrow. Seize the day."* (Luke 9:62 - Message) May we be bold and courageous, knowing that the Lord is with us every step of the way.

Revelation 21:8 reminds us that we must be willing to go through all kinds of oppositions, temptations, trials, and tribulations. In this world, we will have tribulation, but we should be of good cheer because Christ has overcome the world. Many are the afflictions of the righteous!

The Lord is with you, Mighty Warrior. There ain't no time for coward soldiers in God's Army. *Swing Your Sword And Let's Go!*

STRATEGY FOUR
WONDER WOMEN PRAY

Author: Taundra D. Williams

The Power of a Praying Woman

Prayer has been the center of my life's journey, a sacred tradition nurtured by the wise teachings of my mother, grandmother, and father. From the tender age of three, I was already conversing with God before the written word could speak to me through the pages of scripture. Each night, nestled under the covers, I would recite: "Now I lay me down to sleep, I pray the Lord my soul to keep. If I should die before I wake, I pray the Lord my soul to take. God bless my whole family, in Jesus' Name - Amen."

As I blossomed from a child into a young woman, my prayer life matured inside of me. I recall the Christmas morning when, at seven years old, my dream of a white and baby blue bicycle—with a bell and a basket adorned with blue flowers—came true. It was a vivid testament that my childhood petitions were being heard. However, as childhood innocence faded, I learned a vital truth: prayer is not about manipulating a divine power to grant wishes; it is about aligning our desires with God's will, and God gave me the desires of my heart! – Whew!!!

Guided by my father's wisdom, I delved deeper into the Psalms, those ancient prayers that seemed to echo my own heart's cries. By age ten, these verses had transformed from mere words to fervent prayers, molding my heart and strengthening my spirit. Today, prayer remains my first ministry. The Psalms, taught to me by my father, mother, and grandmothers, continue to be a source of strength, and their timeless truths provide solace and joy irrespective of life's storms.

Hannah: A Wonder Woman Who Prayed

The Bible introduces us to a remarkable Wonder Woman named Hannah, as described in (1 Samuel 1:1-20). Barrenness had etched a deep wound in her heart, magnified by a society that valued women primarily for their ability to bear children. Her rival, Peninnah, tormented her relentlessly, reminding Hannah of her emptiness. Despite this, Hannah did not succumb to despair; she turned her pain into power through fervent prayer.

Hannah's story is not just about her longing for a child; it is a narrative of unwavering faith, persistent prayer, and the incredible power of surrender. Let's explore the strategies that can inspire our own prayer lives, particularly when the burdens of our hearts feel overwhelming:

Strategies For Powerful Prayer

Tears as a Weapon: In her anguish, Hannah wept bitterly before the Lord (1 Sam 1:10). These were not just tears of sorrow but of profound longing and a heartfelt plea for divine intervention. Scripture reminds us that God is intimately aware of our sufferings and collects our tears (Ps 56:8). Let your tears flow as a form of prayer, allowing them to wash away despair and usher in God's comforting truths. I remember many times I kneeled to pray, and all that came out were tears. Sometimes, you may not have the words. Sometimes all you can say is —**Lord, Have Mercy! —Lord Help ME! —Lord, You Know!** Sometimes, the anguishing tears of surrender, sorrow, and sadness are all you have. And the great thing about our God is that he understands every moan, groan, tear, muffled scream, and stammering murmur! Hallelujah! Sometimes, all you have to do is **BOW THE KNEE**, just like the song says! It says, — Bow the knee; Trust the heart of your Father when the answer goes beyond what you can see. Bow the knee; Lift your eyes toward heaven and believe the One who holds eternity. And when you don't understand the purpose of His plan, in the King's presence, **BOW THE KNEE!**

Specificity in Supplication: Hannah was specific in her prayers, asking for a son whom she vowed to dedicate to God's service (1 Sam 1:11). While our specific requests might not always be granted as we envision, approaching God with clear petitions demonstrates our trust in His wisdom and timing. Yet, it is vital to remain open to God's plans, acknowledging that His ways surpass our understanding (Isa 55:8-9). Think about this for a moment. When we pray, we know Our Heavenly Father hears us, but the thing about him answering us just like we asked has to be in his will.

From Desperation to Surrender: Over time, Hannah's prayers transformed from desperate pleas to surrendering her desires to God's will. This act of surrender—letting go of our control and trusting in God's sovereignty—is a powerful form of worship (Prov 3:5-6). It frees us from the burden of our expectations and aligns us with God's greater purposes for our lives.

The Persistence Of A Wonder Woman

The Bible doesn't specify how long Hannah prayed for a child, but it highlights her consistency in prayer.

Her persistence teaches us that we must continue communicating with God, even when answers seem delayed, or our desires are unmet. Remember, "The effective, fervent prayer of a righteous man avails much" (James 5:16 NKJV).

Faith-Filled Action: After praying, Hannah did not just sit back; she got up and engaged with life with renewed vigor (1 Sam 1:18). Our prayers should similarly inspire us to action, reinforcing our faith with deeds that reflect our trust in God's ongoing work in our lives (James 2:17).

Overcoming Enemies of Purpose Through Prayer

Doubt: Like Hannah, we may face doubts about God's plan for our lives. But through prayer, we bring these doubts to God, allowing His truth to overcome our uncertainties.

Unbelief: When we struggle to believe, prayer becomes our lifeline to faith. As we communicate with God, He strengthens our belief in His promises and character.

Past Hurts: Hannah's pain from her barrenness and ridicule was healed through prayer. Similarly, we can bring our past traumas to God, allowing His loving presence to heal our wounds.

As Wonder Women of God, we must recognize that our battles are not against flesh and blood but against spiritual forces of evil (Eph 6:12). Prayer is our most potent weapon in this spiritual warfare. When we pray, we engage in combat against the enemy's schemes and align ourselves with God's power and purposes.

"For though we walk in the flesh, we do not war according to the flesh. For the weapons of our warfare are not carnal but mighty in God for pulling down strongholds" (2 Cor 10:3-4 NKJV). Our prayers have the power to demolish arguments and pretensions that set themselves up against the knowledge of God.

Cultivating a Rich Prayer Life

Lessons from Hannah: Hannah's story offers profound insights into cultivating a rich prayer life.

Her journey from anguish to answered prayer exemplifies the transformative power of persistent, honest communication with God.

Creating Sacred Spaces: Like Hannah at the temple, we can designate special places for prayer. This doesn't require an elaborate setup; a quiet corner in your home can become your personal sanctuary. Here, free from distractions, you can pour out your heart to God as Hannah did.

Raw Honesty in Prayer: Hannah's prayers were unfiltered expressions of her pain and longing. She didn't mask her emotions or soften her requests. This teaches us the value of authenticity in our conversations with God. He knows our hearts; we shouldn't hide our true feelings from Him.

Consistency and Persistence: Hannah's regular visits to the temple for prayer demonstrate the importance of consistency. Establishing a daily prayer routine, whether morning, noon, or night, helps build a strong prayer life. Even when answers seem delayed, persist in prayer, remembering that "The effective, fervent prayer of a righteous man avails much" (James 5:16 NKJV).

Listening and Discernment: After pouring out her heart, Hannah was receptive to Eli's words of blessing. In our prayer times, we should also include moments of silence, listening for God's gentle whispers and discerning His guidance.

Expectant Faith: Hannah left the temple changed, full of hope and peace. Approach your prayers with similar expectancy, believing that God hears and will respond according to His perfect will and timing.

Praying Scripture: While not explicitly mentioned in Hannah's story, incorporating God's Word into our prayers can deepen our connection with Him. Use verses that resonate with your situation as a prayer foundation, allowing the living Word to shape your petitions and praises.

Community Prayer: Hannah participated in yearly sacrifices with her family, reminding us of the power of corporate prayer. Find opportunities to pray both individually and with others, strengthening your faith through communal worship and intercession.

Journaling Your Journey: Consider keeping a prayer journal to record your prayers, thoughts, and God's responses. Over time, this journal can become a powerful testament to God's faithfulness and work in your life.

Gratitude and Praise: Hannah's song of thanksgiving after Samuel's birth (1 Sam 2:1-10) underscores the importance of gratitude in our prayer lives. Cultivate a habit of praising God and expressing thankfulness, even before you see the answers to your prayers.

Dedicating Your Blessings: Hannah followed through on her vow to dedicate Samuel to God's service. When God answers your prayers, consider using those blessings to serve Him and others, continuing the cycle of blessing and gratitude.

The Armor of Prayer

As you step onto the battlefield of life, clothe yourself with the armor of prayer—a powerful tool that shields you and fortifies your soul. Prayer is not merely a ritual or a hopeful utterance into the void; it is your direct line to divine power, wisdom, and comfort. It is through prayer that you find the strength to face the tumults (as in commotion. a state of noisy, confused activity) of life with a steady heart and a focused mind.

As Wonder Women of God, we must recognize that our battles are not against flesh and blood but against spiritual forces of evil (Eph 6:12). Prayer is our most potent weapon in this spiritual warfare. When we pray, we engage in combat against the enemy's schemes and align ourselves with God's power and purposes.

The Belt of Truth: In prayer, we fasten the belt of truth around us. This truth is God's Word, which grounds us in reality and dispels the lies of the enemy. Like Hannah, who held onto God's promises despite her circumstances, we, too, must cling to God's truth in our prayers.

The Breastplate of Righteousness: As we pray, we put on the breastplate of righteousness. This isn't our own righteousness but Christ's righteousness given to us. It protects our hearts from condemnation and gives us confidence to boldly approach God's throne of grace.

Shield of Faith: Let faith be your shield against the arrows of doubt and despair. When you pray, you activate this shield, deflecting the trials that seek to weaken your resolve and rob you of your peace.

Sword of the Spirit: The Word of God is your sword, sharp and precise. As you engage in prayer, let the scriptures guide your thoughts and actions. They are the words that cut through deception and confusion, revealing truth and wisdom in every situation.

Helmet of Salvation: Keep your mind guarded with the helmet of salvation. Your identity as a redeemed child of God should dominate your thoughts, driving away fears and insecurities. In prayer, reaffirm your status as His beloved, knowing that no spiritual battle can strip you of this eternal truth.

Boots of Readiness: Prepare yourself with the boots of readiness that come from the gospel of peace. Stand firm in the good news of Christ, which equips you to walk in love and peace, even across the roughest terrains of conflict or adversity.

In Times Of Spiritual Attack, We Can Pray

"Lord, I put on the whole armor of God, that I may stand against the wiles of the devil" (Eph 6:11).

"God, gird my waist with truth, cover my chest with the breastplate of righteousness, and shod my feet with the preparation of the gospel of peace" (Eph 6:14-15).

"Father, I take up the shield of faith to quench all the fiery darts of the wicked one. I put on the helmet of salvation and take the sword of the Spirit, which is Your Word" (Eph 6:16-17).

"Holy Spirit, pray through me with all prayer and supplication, keeping me watchful with all perseverance" (Eph 6:18).

Remember, ***"No weapon formed against you shall prosper, and every tongue which rises against you in judgment You shall condemn"*** **(Isa 54:17 NKJV).**

Our prayers activate these promises, turning them into shields of protection and swords of victory.

Embrace the Wonder Woman Within

You are fearfully and wonderfully made by God (Ps 139:14). Every strand of your being was crafted with divine intention and care. Your strength is not just in the muscles you build or the intellectual prowess you wield but in the very essence of your spirit, infused with God's breath of life.

The battles you face are not mere obstacles but opportunities for growth and testimony to your faith. Each challenge, whether a personal struggle, a professional setback, or a spiritual dilemma, serves to refine your character, forging you into a warrior of strength, resilience, and unwavering faith. Like the skilled hands of a blacksmith, God uses these challenges to shape you, to refine your spirit in the fiery trials, making you stronger and more resilient.

The Journey Continues

As we close this chapter, let us remember that the journey of prayer is not a path with a final destination but an ongoing voyage that enriches and transforms us continuously. Each step you take in your prayer life deepens your connection with God, fortifying you as a Wonder Woman armed with faith.

Every moment spent in prayer is a thread woven into the fabric of your spiritual life, strengthening the bond between your earthly journey and divine destiny.

So, let us not grow weary. The journey continues, and with each step, let us press on with perseverance and passion. The road may be long and, at times, arduous, but it is lined with the presence of God, the support of fellow believers, and the echoes of prayers that have shaped generations. Arm yourself daily with the armor of God, stepping boldly into each day with prayer as your guide and faith as your shield.

STRATEGY FIVE
SHE BELIEVED SHE COULD, SO SHE DID

Author: Prophet Apryl Essien

Introduction

In the labyrinth of human suffering, where shadows of trauma and despair loom large, the journey toward healing and redemption is often fraught with obstacles and uncertainties. For many, the scars of childhood sexual abuse and rejection cast a long and suffocating shadow over their lives, shaping the contours of their existence and clouding the path toward wholeness and liberation. In the crucible of my journey, I found solace and inspiration in the timeless wisdom of ancient texts, drawing strength from the narratives of courage, resilience, and divine deliverance

The Inspiration of Jael

A Biblical Heroine: Amidst the tapestry of biblical lore, one figure emerged as a beacon of hope—a figure whose story resonated deeply within the recesses of my soul: Jael. In the annals of the book of Judges, amidst the tumultuous landscape of ancient Israel, Jael's narrative unfolds as a testament to the transformative power of resilience and agency in the face of adversity. As I grappled with the echoes of childhood sexual abuse and rejection, I found solace and guidance in the footsteps of this remarkable woman—a woman whose courage and cunning defied convention and whose actions echoed through the corridors of time.

Finding Strength in Ancient Wisdom: Yet, amidst the trials and tribulations of my journey, it was not only the example of Jael that illuminated my path but also the unwavering presence of a divine deliverer—a source of strength and solace in the darkest of hours.

In the embrace of God's grace, I discovered a refuge—a sanctuary of healing and redemption where the wounds of the past could be transmuted into sources of empowerment and renewal.

This chapter serves as a testament to the transformative power of faith, resilience, and divine intervention—a chronicle of triumph over adversity, of light emerging from the shadows, and of hope reborn amidst the ashes of despair. Through the prism of Jael's narrative and the guiding hand of God, I invite you to embark on a journey of self-discovery and empowerment—a journey that transcends the boundaries of time and space, uniting us in our shared humanity and collective quest for healing and wholeness.

In the pages that follow, I will recount the harrowing chapters of my journey—a journey marked by pain, rejection, and the indomitable pursuit of healing. From the depths of despair to the pinnacle of triumph, I will trace the contours of my evolution—a metamorphosis shaped by the crucible of adversity and illuminated by the guiding light of faith and resilience.

Setting the Stage: Jael's Story

But before delving into the depths of my narrative, it is imperative to set the stage—to illuminate the figure of Jael and unravel the tapestry of her story. Within the annals of biblical lore, Jael emerges as a figure of unparalleled strength—a woman whose actions would be celebrated and vilified in equal measure. In her story, I found echoes of my own struggle—the struggle to confront the forces of darkness, to reclaim agency in the face of adversity, and to emerge triumphant in the shadow of despair.

The Historical Context: In the book of Judges, amidst the tumultuous landscape of ancient Israel, we encounter a nation besieged by adversity—a people grappling with the specter of oppression and the relentless tide of injustice. It is within this crucible of chaos that the figure of Jael emerges—a woman of humble origins, yet she possessed strength and resolve that defied convention.

A Moment of Destiny: As the Israelites rallied against their oppressors, led by the valiant warrior Barak and the Prophet Deborah, Jael's moment of destiny unfolded—a moment that would alter the course of history and resonate with timeless resonance. In the aftermath of the battle, as Sisera, the commander of the Canaanite army, sought refuge in her tent, Jael seized upon the opportunity presented to her—a chance to confront the forces of oppression and reclaim agency in the face of adversity.

In the climactic moment of their encounter, Jael offered Sisera solace and sanctuary—a gesture of hospitality that belied the simmering undercurrent of tension and conflict. And yet, as Sisera succumbed to the embrace of sleep, Jael seized upon the moment with decisive resolve, driving a tent peg through his temple and delivering a fatal blow to the forces of tyranny.

Controversy and Interpretation: In the aftermath of her actions, Jael emerged as a figure of controversy—a woman whose deeds would be celebrated and vilified in equal measure. To some, she was hailed as a heroine—a champion of justice and liberation—whose courage and cunning toppled the forces of oppression. To others, she was reviled as a traitor—a figure of betrayal and deceit, whose actions defied easy categorization and challenged conventional notions of morality.

Personal Reflection and Parallel

And yet, amidst the cacophony of voices and the clash of interpretations, one truth remained immutable: the story of Jael resonated with timeless resonance—a testament to the enduring power of courage, resilience, and the indomitable spirit of human agency.

As I reflect on the narrative of Jael, I am struck by the parallels that resonate with my journey—a journey marked by the scars of trauma, the echoes of rejection, and the relentless pursuit of healing and redemption. In Jael, I see echoes of my struggle—the struggle to confront the forces of darkness, to reclaim agency in the face of adversity, and to emerge triumphant in the shadow of despair.

Together, we will embark on a journey of healing and empowerment—a journey that transcends the boundaries of time and space, uniting us in our shared humanity and collective quest for wholeness. Through the lens of Jael's narrative and the unwavering presence of a divine deliverer, we will uncover the hidden reservoirs of strength and resilience that lie dormant within us, waiting to be unleashed in the pursuit of healing and liberation.

As we journey forth, may we find solace in the timeless wisdom of ancient texts, drawing inspiration from the courage and resolve of those who have gone before us. May we, like Jael, rise to meet the challenges that lie ahead, forging a path of hope and healing in the wake of adversity.

This is the story of Jael. This is my story. And together, guided by the unwavering hand of God, may we discover the boundless depths of our own resilience and the transformative power of faith in the face of adversity.

A Journey of Healing

Confronting Childhood Trauma: In the depths of childhood trauma, where shadows of abuse and rejection loomed large, I found solace and strength in the story of Jael from the Bible. Like her, I faced daunting challenges, navigating a world tainted by pain and betrayal. Yet, through the lens of faith and the guiding hand of God, I discovered the path to healing and deliverance.

Echoes of Abuse and Rejection: Growing up, my innocence was shattered by the insidious grip of sexual abuse and the sting of relentless rejection. Each day seemed like a battlefield where my sense of self-worth was battered and bruised. The scars of my past weighed heavily on my heart, casting dark shadows over my present and clouding my vision of the future.

In the midst of despair, the story of Jael emerged as a beacon of hope and inspiration. Jael, a woman of courage and conviction, faced her trials with unwavering faith and determination. When the oppressive forces of Sisera threatened to engulf her people, she rose to the challenge, embracing her role as an instrument of divine deliverance.

Similarly, I found myself confronted by the giants of my trauma, their presence casting a long shadow over my life. Yet, like Jael, I refused to succumb to despair. Instead, I clung to the promise of redemption, trusting in the unwavering love of a God who hears the cries of the oppressed and offers refuge to the brokenhearted.

The Pathway to Deliverance: With each passing day, I embarked on a journey of self-discovery and healing, guided by the timeless wisdom found within the pages of Scripture. Through prayer and reflection, I unearthed the strength within me, tapping into reservoirs of resilience I never knew existed. Like Jael, I embraced my identity as a beloved child of God, fearlessly confronting the demons of my past and reclaiming the narrative of my life.

In the face of adversity, I found empowerment in Jael's unwavering resolve, and her willingness to confront the enemy head-on and emerge victorious against all odds. Armed with faith as my shield and determination as my sword, I confronted the specter of abuse and rejection with newfound courage and conviction.

Yet, my journey toward healing was not without its challenges. There were moments of doubt and despair where the weight of my past threatened to engulf me once more. In those dark hours, I turned to God as my deliverer, drawing strength from His promises and finding solace in His unfailing love.

The Power of Faith and Resilience

Transforming Scars into Strength: Through prayer and reflection, I began to see the scars of my past not as marks of shame but as testaments to the resilience of the human spirit. Like Jael, I embraced my scars as symbols of triumph, reminders of the battles I had fought and the victories I had won.

In the embrace of God's grace, I found the courage to confront the wounds of my past and embrace the journey toward healing. With each step forward, I felt the chains of my trauma loosening their grip, replaced by a newfound sense of freedom and wholeness.

As I stand on the threshold of a new chapter in my life, I am reminded of Jael's legacy of courage and faith. Her story serves as a testament to the transformative power of faith in the face of adversity, a reminder that no challenge is insurmountable in the light of God's love.

The Role of Forgiveness: Through the trials and tribulations of my journey, I have come to realize that true healing begins with forgiveness—forgiveness for others, forgiveness for myself, and ultimately, forgiveness for the past that once held me captive.

Embracing a New Identity: In the end, it is not the scars of our past that define us, but the strength of our spirit and the depth of our faith. Like Jael, I have emerged from the ashes of my past, a living testament to the redemptive power of God's love. As I continue on this journey of healing and restoration, I am grateful for the unwavering presence of a God who walks beside me, guiding me toward a future filled with hope, healing, and wholeness.

In the depths of despair, amidst the echoes of childhood trauma, I found redemption and renewal through the timeless wisdom of Scripture and the unwavering love of God. The story of Jael, a woman of courage and conviction, resonated deeply within my soul, offering a glimmer of hope in the darkest of nights.

Through her example, I learned that true strength lies not in the absence of fear but in the willingness to confront it head-on, armed with the shield of faith and the sword of truth. Like Jael, I faced my battles with courage and determination, refusing to be defined by the scars of my past.

In the embrace of God's grace, I discovered the power of forgiveness—a balm for the wounded soul, a pathway to healing and wholeness. Through forgiveness, I found liberation from the chains of resentment and bitterness, reclaiming my identity as a beloved child of God.

As I reflect on the journey that brought me to this moment, I am filled with gratitude for the guiding hand of Providence, which has led me through the valleys of despair and into the light of redemption. Though the road was fraught with obstacles, God remained steadfast in His love, a beacon of hope shining brightly in the darkness.

A Message of Hope

From Survival to Triumph: Let my story be a beacon of hope, a testament to the resilience of the human spirit. In the face of unimaginable pain and suffering, I dared to believe that I could overcome the shadows of my past, and with unwavering faith in God, I did.

Childhood sexual abuse and rejection cast long shadows over my formative years, leaving behind scars that seemed impossible to heal. The weight of shame and despair threatened to engulf me, suffocating any semblance of hope or joy. Yet, in the depths of my despair, a flicker of light pierced through the darkness—the promise of redemption, the assurance of deliverance.

With each passing day, I clung to the belief that I was more than the sum of my past traumas, that I was worthy of love and belonging. As I journeyed through the labyrinth of healing, I discovered the power of faith – a beacon of hope guiding me through the storm.

Through prayer, I found solace in the embrace of a God who sees the brokenness of our hearts and offers healing to the wounded soul. In His presence, I discovered the strength to confront the demons of my past and to reclaim my identity as a beloved child of God.

Belief became my lifeline and my anchor amid life's tempests. With faith as my shield and determination as my sword, I confronted the specter of abuse and rejection with unwavering resolve. And though the journey was fraught with challenges and setbacks, I pressed onward, fueled by the conviction that victory was within reach.

Today, as I stand on the mountaintop of healing, I am humbled by the journey that brought me here. My story is not just one of survival but of triumph—a testament to the transformative power of faith and the boundless grace of God.

Encouragement for Fellow Survivors: Let my story be a source of encouragement to you, dear friend. Whatever trials you may face, whatever demons may haunt your past, know that you are not alone. With faith as your compass and God as your guide, you too can overcome the darkest of nights and emerge into the light of a new dawn.

The Power of Belief: Believe that you are worthy of love and belonging. Believe that you are stronger than you know. And above all, believe that with God by your side, all things are possible. In the end, it is not the trials we face that define us, but the strength of our spirit and the depth of our faith.

Dear sister, let my story encourage you. I want you to believe one day, you too can and will stand as a testament to the power of faith and the triumph of the human spirit. And so, as I stand on the threshold of a new beginning, I offer this prayer:

Let Us Pray

Father, In the quiet moments of reflection, I come before you with a heart overflowing with gratitude. You have been my rock and my refuge, my strength in times of weakness, and my deliverer in moments of despair. Through the storms of life, your love has remained constant, a beacon of hope illuminating the path before me.

Lord, I thank you for the story of Jael, a woman of courage and faith who faced her trials with unwavering resolve. Through her example, you have shown me the power of perseverance and the triumph of faith over adversity. Like Jael, I have confronted the giants of my own past, trusting in your promise of redemption and restoration. In the quiet corners of my heart, I have wrestled with the pain of childhood trauma—the scars of abuse and rejection that threatened to define me. Yet, in your infinite mercy, you have turned my wounds into sources of strength, my brokenness into vessels of healing.

Father, I pray for all those who have walked a similar path – for the wounded souls who bear the weight of past hurts, for the broken spirits longing for redemption. May they find solace in your presence, strength in your promises, and healing in your embrace. As I journey forward, Lord, I ask for the courage to forgive – to release the burdens of bitterness and resentment that weigh heavy on my soul. Grant me the grace to extend compassion to those who have wronged me, and the wisdom to walk in the path of righteousness. In your hands, O Lord, I place my past, my present, and my future. Guide me, protect me, and lead me in the way everlasting. May the story of my redemption be a testament to your unfailing love and a beacon of hope for all who seek refuge in your arms.

With a heart full of faith and a spirit renewed, I step boldly into the future, trusting in the promise of God's unfailing love. For in Him, I have found deliverance, redemption, and everlasting hope.

In Jesus' name, Amen.

Scriptures of Encouragement

Here are several Bible verses that can provide comfort, encouragement, and hope during times of trauma and healing.

1. ***Isaiah 41:10 (NIV):*** "So do not fear, for I am with you; do not be dismayed, for I am your God. I will strengthen you and help you; I will uphold you with my righteous right hand."
2. ***Psalm 34:18 (NIV):*** "The Lord is close to the brokenhearted and saves those who are crushed in spirit."

3. ***Psalm 147:3 (NIV):*** "He heals the brokenhearted and binds up their wounds."

4. ***Matthew 11:28-30: (NIV):*** "Come to me, all you who are weary and burdened, and I will give you rest. Take my yoke upon you and learn from me, for I am gentle and humble in heart, and you will find rest for your souls. For my yoke is easy and my burden is light."

5. ***Romans 8:28 (NIV):*** "And we know that in all things God works for the good of those who love him, who have been called according to his purpose."

6. ***2 Corinthians 1:3-4 (NIV):*** "Praise be to the God and Father of our Lord Jesus Christ, the Father of compassion and the God of all comfort, who comforts us in all our troubles, so that we can comfort those in any trouble with the comfort we ourselves receive from God."

7. ***Philippians 4:6-7 (NIV):*** "Do not be anxious about anything, but in every situation, by prayer and petition, with thanksgiving, present your requests to God. And the peace of God, which transcends all understanding, will guard your hearts and your minds in Christ Jesus."
8. ***1 Peter 5:7 (NIV):*** "Cast all your anxiety on him because he cares for you."

May these verses can serve as a source of strength, hope, and comfort during times of trauma and healing, reminding us of God's love, compassion, and faithfulness.

STRATEGY SIX
NO MORE EXCUSES

Author: Taundra D. Williams

Introduction

In our journey as Wonder Women of Faith, we often encounter obstacles that seem insurmountable. These internal or external barriers can become convenient excuses that hold us back from fulfilling our God-given purpose. But what if we chose to say, "No more excuses"? What if we decided to step out in faith despite our fears, our past, or the opinions of others?

Unleashing the Wonder Woman Within

Ladies, it's time to suit up, not in a cape or a golden lasso, but in the full armor of God. It's time to embrace your inner Wonder Woman – not the fictional character, but the wonder-full woman God created you to be. This chapter isn't just about making excuses; it's about recognizing the Shero that God has placed within each of us and letting her soar.

Have you ever felt that nudge in your spirit, that soft whisper calling you to step out in faith, only to find yourself frozen in place, a thousand reasons why you "can't" flooding your mind? I've been there, and I bet you have too. We're not alone in this struggle. In fact, we're in pretty good company. Even some of the greatest Wonder Women of our faith grappled with the same doubts and excuses when God called them to action.

In this chapter, we're going to tackle those excuses head-on. We'll dive into the story of Moses, a man who had a list of reasons why he wasn't the right person for the job when God called him. Sound familiar? But here's the thing: God didn't accept

Moses' excuses, and He doesn't accept ours either. It's time for us, as women of faith, as modern-day Wonder Women, to lay down our excuses and pick up the sword of the Spirit, ready to answer God's call with a resounding "Yes!"

Before we jump into Moses' story, let's remind ourselves of the spiritual armor we're called to put on – our Wonder Woman suit, if you will: "Finally, be strong in the Lord and in his mighty power. Put on the full armor of God so that you can take your stand against the devil's schemes. For our struggle is not against flesh and blood, but against the rulers, against the authorities, against the powers of this dark world, and against the spiritual forces of evil in the heavenly realms. Therefore put on the full armor of God so that when the day of evil comes, you may be able to stand your ground, and after you have done everything, to stand. Stand firm then, with the belt of truth buckled around your waist, with the breastplate of righteousness in place, and with your feet fitted with the readiness that comes from the gospel of peace. In addition to all this, take up the shield of faith, with which you can extinguish all the flaming arrows of the evil one. Take the helmet of salvation and the sword of the Spirit, which is the word of God." (Ephesians 6:10-17, NIV)

This armor isn't just for show. It's not a costume we put on for Sunday service. It's our daily gear, our protection, and our weapon in spiritual warfare. And make no mistake, making excuses when God calls us is a form of spiritual warfare. It's the enemy whispering doubts, feeding our insecurities, and trying to keep us from stepping into our God-given purpose as Wonder Women of faith.

So, let's get real. Let's examine our excuses through the lens of Moses' story and learn how to overcome them. It's time to silence the voice of fear and amplify the voice of faith. Are you ready to unleash your inner Wonder Woman? Let's dive in.

The Call: When God Interrupts Your Ordinary

Picture this: You're going about your day doing the same old routine you've done a thousand times before. Maybe you're folding laundry, or sitting in traffic, or herding your kids to school. And then, out of nowhere, God shows up. He doesn't just show up; He shows off, making it crystal clear that He's got something big in mind for you. It's your Wonder Woman moment – the moment when God calls you out of the ordinary into the extraordinary.

That's exactly what happened to Moses. He was just doing his job, tending his father-in-law's flock, when suddenly:

"There, the angel of the Lord appeared to him in flames of fire from within a bush. Moses saw that though the bush was on fire, it did not burn up. So

Moses thought, 'I will go over and see this strange sight—why the bush does not burn up.'" (Exodus 3:2-3, NIV)

God had Moses' attention, and He has ours sometimes, too. Maybe it's not through a burning bush but through a persistent thought, a recurring dream, or a series of "coincidences" that are too perfect to be chance. When God calls, it's rarely convenient, seldom expected, and almost always intimidating. But it's in these moments that our inner Wonder Woman is awakened.

Think about these Wonder Women in the Bible.

Esther was just a young girl when she was suddenly called to save her people.

Mary was a humble virgin when an angel appeared and told her she would bear the Son of God.

Deborah was living her life when God called her to be a prophet and judge over Israel.

Each of these women had their ordinary interrupted by God's extraordinary call.

But here's the thing: God's call on your life isn't a suggestion. It's not a "Hey, if you're not too busy" kind of request. It's a divine appointment, a holy interruption to your ordinary. And just like Moses, just like Esther and Mary and Deborah, we have a choice to make when God calls: Will we step up, will we let our inner Wonder Woman rise, or will we start making excuses?

Excuse #1: *"Who Am I?"*

When God laid out His plan to use Moses to lead the Israelites out of Egypt, Moses' first response was:

"Who am I that I should go to Pharaoh and bring the Israelites out of Egypt?" (Exodus 3:11, NIV)

Can you relate? I know I can. How many times have we looked at a challenge before us and thought, "Who am I to do this? I'm not qualified. I'm not good enough. I'm just... me." This is the kryptonite to our inner Wonder Woman—the inadequacy trap.

This is the enemy's favorite tool. He loves to remind us of our shortcomings, our past failures, and our current struggles. He wants us to focus on our **"Who Am I"** instead of God's **"I AM."**

But look at God's response to Moses:

"I will be with you." (Exodus 3:12, NIV)

God doesn't argue with Moses about his qualifications. He doesn't list out Moses' resume or remind him of his princely education in Egypt.

Instead, He offers the only qualification that matters: His presence.

The truth is we are inadequate on our own. But that's the point. God doesn't call the qualified; He qualifies the called. Your **"Who Am I"** is exactly why God can use you. It's in our weakness that His strength is perfect (2 Corinthians 12:9).

Think about the Wonder Women in your life—your mother who raised you against all odds, your friend who battled cancer with unwavering faith, and your coworker who stands firm in her beliefs in a challenging work environment. They probably didn't feel qualified for their challenges either, but God's strength shone through their perceived weaknesses.

So the next time you feel that nudge to step out in faith and you hear that whisper of "Who am I?", remember: You are a daughter of the King. You are chosen, called, and equipped by the God of the universe. And most importantly, He is with you. You are a Wonder Woman in His eyes, capable of far more than you can imagine through His power working in you.

Excuse #2: *"What If They Don't Believe Me?"*

After getting past his initial feelings of inadequacy, Moses voiced another concern: ***"What if they do not believe me or listen to me and say, 'The Lord did not appear to you'?" (Exodus 4:1, NIV)***

Ah, the fear of rejection. It's a universal human experience, but for those of us answering God's call, it can be paralyzing. What if people don't take us seriously? What if they question our motives or doubt our sincerity? This fear can keep our inner Wonder Woman hidden, afraid to stand out and speak up.

God's response to Moses was practical and powerful. He gave Moses three miraculous signs to perform: turning his staff into a snake, making his hand leprous and then healing it, and turning water from the Nile into blood (Exodus 4:2-9). These signs weren't just party tricks; they were tangible proof of God's power working through Moses.

While we might not have the same miraculous signs at our disposal, we do have something equally powerful: our testimony. The change God has wrought in our lives, the battles He's brought us through, the grace He's shown us – these are our "signs and wonders."

"They triumphed over him by the blood of the Lamb and by the word of their testimony; they did not love their lives so much as to shrink from death." (Revelation 12:11, NIV)

Your story, your journey of faith, is a powerful weapon against rejection. It's a firsthand account of God's faithfulness that no one can deny or take away from you. Every Wonder Woman has a story of God's work in her life, and that story has the power to change lives.

Moreover, remember that your call isn't about winning a popularity contest. It's about obedience to God. People rejected Jesus, the perfect Son of God. If we face rejection for following Him, we're in good company.

"If the world hates you, keep in mind that it hated me first." (John 15:18, NIV)

Think about the Wonder Women throughout history who faced rejection but pressed on anyway.

Joan of Arc was mocked and ultimately martyred for following God's call.

Mother Teresa faced criticism and skepticism but continued to serve the poorest of the poor.

Harriet Tubman risked her life and freedom to lead others to freedom, despite the danger of rejection and betrayal.

So when the fear of rejection rears its ugly head, remind yourself: **YOUR APPROVAL COMES FROM GOD, NOT PEOPLE. YOUR MISSION IS OBEDIENCE, NOT POPULARITY**, and your testimony is more powerful than you know.

Excuse #3: "I'm Not Eloquent"

Even after God addressed his first two concerns, Moses wasn't done making excuses: *"Moses said to the Lord, 'Pardon your servant, Lord. I have never been eloquent, neither in the past nor since you have spoken to your servant. I am slow of speech and tongue."* **(Exodus 4:10, NIV)**

This excuse hits close to home for many of us. How often have we held back from sharing our faith, leading a Bible study, or stepping into a leadership role because we didn't think we were "good enough" at speaking? This self-doubt can be a formidable enemy to our inner Wonder Woman.

But God's response to Moses is a game-changer: "The Lord said to him, 'Who gave human beings their mouths? Who makes them deaf or mute? Who gives them sight or makes them blind? Is it not I, the Lord? Now go; I will help you speak and will teach you what to say.'" (Exodus 4:11-12, NIV)

God reminds Moses (and us) of a fundamental truth: He is the creator of our abilities and the enabler of our inabilities. If He has called you to a task, He will equip you for it. Your perceived weaknesses are opportunities for God's strength to shine through.

Remember, these Wonder Women in the Bible weren't known for their eloquence:

Esther was terrified to speak to the king, but her words saved a nation.

Mary wasn't a great orator, but her simple "YES" to God brought forth the Savior of The WORLD!

Look at *The Samaritan Woman* at the well. She wasn't a trained evangelist, but by sharing her testimony with others, her words brought her whole town to Jesus.

And yet God used each of these women mightily. Why? Because they chose to trust God's ability more than they doubted their own inability.

Listen, God's power often works best through our weaknesses: "But he said to me, 'My grace is sufficient for you, for my power is made perfect in weakness.' Therefore I will boast all the more gladly about my weaknesses, so that Christ's power may rest on me." (2 Corinthians 12:9, NIV)

Think about the Wonder Women you saw on the stages during She Visions or if you are new to this movement, consider the women you go to see speak or you follow on social media. Chances are, they're not all polished public speakers or charismatic leaders. Maybe to you we look like we are, but the truth is we sometimes battle with insecurities and so we understand that it is not our will, but the Master will be done. But we said yes to God despite our fears and insecurities and we move out of the way to allow God's strength to shine through our weaknesses.

So the next time you feel tempted to use the "I'm not good enough" excuse, remember: God doesn't call the equipped, He equips the called. Your weaknesses are not obstacles to God; they're opportunities for Him to display His power. It's time to embrace your inner Wonder Woman, imperfections, and all.

Excuse #4: "Send Someone Else"

After all of God's reassurances, Moses makes one final, desperate attempt to get out of his calling:

"But Moses said, 'Pardon your servant, Lord. Please send someone else.'" (Exodus 4:13, NIV)

I can't help but be tickled at Moses responses, while he is so polite to the Master. Isn't this how we are? Um, excuse me Lord, I am not saying you made a mistake, but I just feel like I need a pass!!!

This is where the rubber meets the road. It's one thing to voice our insecurities and doubts; it's another to flat-out refuse God's call. Yet how many of us have been here? We've run out of specific excuses, so we just plead, "Not me, Lord. Someone else would be better suited for this." It's the final barrier keeping our inner Wonder Woman from stepping into the light.

It's at this point that we see God's patience has limits: "Then the Lord's anger burned against Moses, and he said, 'What about your brother, Aaron the Levite? I know he can speak well. He is already on his way to meet you, and he will be glad to see you.'" (Exodus 4:14, NIV)

God doesn't let Moses off the hook. Instead, He provides a partner, someone to come alongside Moses in his mission.

This teaches us an important lesson: God's call on our lives often involves community. We're not meant to go alone. Even Wonder Woman had her *Justice League!*

But notice that God doesn't replace Moses with Aaron. Moses is still central to the plan. God accommodates Moses' weakness by providing strength through a partner, but He doesn't excuse Moses from the call.

This reluctance to commit often stems from a misunderstanding of God's call. We think it's about our comfort, our convenience, our plans. But God's call is about His kingdom, His glory, and His plans.

"For I know the plans I have for you," declares the Lord, "plans to prosper you and not to harm you, plans to give you hope and a future." (Jeremiah 29:11, NIV)

God's plans for us are good, even when they're challenging. Saying yes to God's call might be scary, but it's always worth it. The adventure of following God, of being part of His grand narrative, far outweighs the temporary comfort of staying in our safe, predictable routines.

Here are more Wonder Women throughout history who said yes to God's call:

Corrie ten Boom, who risked her life to hide Jews during World War II.

Amy Carmichael, who left her comfortable life to serve as a missionary in India for 55 years without furlough.

Rosa Parks, who said yes to standing up (or sitting down) for justice, sparking a movement.

These women weren't fearless – they were faithful. They chose to say YES to God's call despite their fears and doubts. They let their inner Wonder Woman rise to the challenge.

Moving Beyond Excuses

So, how do we move past these excuses and step boldly into God's call on our lives? How do we unleash our inner Wonder Woman? Here are some practical steps:

1. ***Recognize The Source Of Your Excuses:*** Most of our excuses are rooted in fear. Identify what you're really afraid of, and bring that fear

to God. Remember, Wonder Woman isn't fearless – she's courageous in the face of fear.

2. ***Remind yourself of God's promises***: When doubts creep in, combat them with God's truth. Memorize scriptures that remind you of God's faithfulness and power. Let God's Word be your golden lasso of truth.

3. ***Start Small***: You don't have to change the world overnight. Take small steps of obedience. Each step builds your faith and confidence. Even Wonder Woman had to learn to fly!

4. ***Find your Justice League***: Don't try to go it alone. Find a community that supports your calling and can come alongside you. Surround yourself with other Wonder Women of faith who can encourage you and pray for you.

5. ***Focus on God, not yourself***: When you feel inadequate, remember that it's not about your

ability but God's. Your power comes from Him, not from yourself.

6. ***Embrace failure as part of the journey:*** Don't let the fear of messing up hold you back. Even Wonder Woman had moments of doubt and failure. Remember, every Shero's or Hero's story includes setbacks and learning experiences. Even Moses made mistakes, but God used him mightily.

7. ***Keep your eyes on the prize:*** Remember the bigger picture. Your obedience to God's call has eternal significance. You're not just fighting earthly battles; you're part of a cosmic struggle for God's kingdom. "Therefore, my dear brothers and sisters, stand firm. Let nothing move you. Always give yourselves fully to the work of the Lord, because you know that your labor in the Lord is not in vain." (1 Corinthians 15:58, NIV)

8. ***Celebrate other Wonder Women***: Look for and celebrate the Wonder Women around you. When you see another woman stepping out in faith, cheer her on. Your encouragement might be just what she needs to keep going.

9. ***Embrace your unique superpowers***: God has given you unique gifts and experiences. Don't compare your calling to others. Your particular blend of talents, personality, and experiences makes you the perfect Wonder Woman for your specific mission.

10. ***Put on your armor daily***: Remember the armor of God we talked about at the beginning? Make putting it on a daily practice. Start each day by intentionally claiming God's truth, righteousness, peace, faith, salvation, and His Word as your protection and power.

Wonder Women in Action: Modern-Day Examples

Here are some modern-day Wonder Women who have embraced God's call on their lives, despite their fears and doubts:

1. *Malala Yousafzai:* This young Pakistani activist stood up for girls' education, even in the face of violent opposition. Her courage and persistence have inspired millions worldwide.
2. *Joni Eareckson Tada:* Despite a diving accident that left her quadriplegic, Joni has become a powerful advocate for people with disabilities, an author, and an artist. Her faith and perseverance have touched countless lives.
3. *Christine Caine:* Overcoming a background of abuse and abandonment, Christine founded A21, a global anti-human trafficking organization. She's a living testament to how God can use our pain for His purposes.

4. ***Katie Davis Majors****:* At 18, Katie moved to Uganda and eventually adopted 13 girls. She founded **Amazima Ministries**, which feeds and educates hundreds of children. Her story reminds us that we're never too young to answer God's call.

5. ***Immaculée Ilibagiza***: A survivor of the Rwandan genocide, Immaculée has become a powerful speaker on faith and forgiveness. Her story shows how God can bring beauty from even the darkest circumstances.

These women aren't Sheros with magical powers. They're ordinary women who said yes to God's extraordinary call. They faced fears, doubts, and seemingly insurmountable obstacles. But they chose to step out in faith, and God has used them in remarkable ways.

No More Excuses – It's Time to Soar

Wonder Women, it's time to lay down our excuses and pick up our swords. It's time to stop focusing on our inadequacies and start focusing on God's adequacy. It's time to silence the voice of fear and amplify the voice of faith. It's time to throw your voice like an arrow.

Remember, you are not defined by your past failures, your current struggles, or your perceived weaknesses. You are defined by your identity in Christ. You are a daughter of the King, chosen and called for such a time as this. You are a Wonder Woman in God's kingdom.

God's call on your life is not a burden to bear but an adventure to embrace. Yes, it will be challenging, and yes, it will push you out of your comfort zone, but it will also be the most fulfilling, exciting journey you could ever embark on.

So the next time you hear God's call and feel those excuses rising up, remember Moses. Remember how God took a reluctant, stuttering shepherd and used him to lead a nation to freedom. Remember the Wonder Women we've talked about – both from the Bible and from our modern world. Remember that the same God who called and equipped them is calling and equipping you.

No more excuses. It's time to say yes to God's call. It's time to step out in faith. It's time to become the Wonder Woman of God you were created to be.

"But those who hope in the Lord will renew their strength. They will soar on wings like eagles; they will run and not grow weary, they will walk and not be faint." (Isaiah 40:31, NIV)

Remember, Wonder Woman, you were born for such a time as this. The world is waiting for you to rise up, to step into your calling, to be the Shero

God created you to be. So put on your armor, take up your sword, and let's change the world—one act of faith at a time. Your mission awaits!

STRATEGY SEVEN
IT'S ALL OR NOTHING!

Author: Carol Hardy

DEDICATION: This is dedicated to the women who have taught me to stand firm on the word of God. To my husband who inspires me and gives me guidance when I can't see the path.

Wielding the Sword of the Spirit

In the vast arsenal of God's warriors, there exists no weapon more potent, more versatile, or more essential than the sword. As we delve into the depths of spiritual warfare and our role as God's chosen fighters, we must first understand the nature and power of our primary weapon. Ephesians 6:17 (GNT) instructs us to "accept salvation as a helmet, and the word of God as the sword which the Spirit gives you."

But what exactly is a sword? In the physical realm, it's a weapon with a long blade for cutting or thrusting. It's often a symbol of honor and authority. When you see a sword, you have an immediate understanding of its potential - its ability to cause harm, to defend, to conquer. Yet, in the spiritual realm, our sword - the Word of God - is infinitely more powerful and multifaceted than any earthly weapon.

King David, a man after God's own heart and a skilled warrior, understood this well. In Psalm 144:1 (Easy), he writes, "Lord, I praise you! You are my rock! My strong rock! You teach me how to fight well. You show me how to use my weapons." David recognized that true skill in spiritual warfare comes not from our own strength or ability, but from the Lord's instruction and guidance.

The true power of the sword, however, is not fully realized until we begin to wield it. When you understand the power of your sword - the living, active Word of God - you will never again bring mere daggers to a sword fight. You'll be equipped for every battle, prepared for every assault of the enemy.

The Evolution of the Sword

To truly appreciate our spiritual weapon, let's explore the history and evolution of the physical sword. This journey takes us back to the very beginning, echoing the words of John 1:1-4 (GNT):

"In the beginning the Word already existed; the Word was with God, and the Word was God. From the very beginning the Word was with God. Through him God made all things; not one thing in all creation was made without him. The Word was the source of life, and this life brought light to people."

Just as the Word has existed from the beginning, so too has the concept of the sword been present throughout human history. The demands of warfare caused the shape and size of swords to evolve over time. As swords evolved, so did the skills required to wield them effectively. Swordsmen had to study, train, refine, and develop their abilities. They had to mature in their craft.

This process of growth and refinement mirrors our own spiritual journey. Every time we open our mouths to speak God's truth, it's a dress rehearsal for the real battles we face. We must continually hone our skills, deepen our understanding of God's Word, and mature in our faith. This ongoing process of refinement is not optional; it's essential for our effectiveness in spiritual warfare.

Interestingly, swords originated from daggers. This evolution reminds us of an important spiritual truth: if you find yourself using a dagger instead of your sword, you've allowed the enemy to come too close. We must maintain our spiritual distance, wielding the full power of God's Word rather than resorting to lesser weapons.

In our spiritual battles, maintaining this distance is crucial. It's about setting boundaries, guarding our hearts, and not allowing the enemy to encroach upon the territory God has given us. When we stay alert and vigilant, wielding our sword skillfully, we keep the enemy at bay and protect the precious ground we've gained in our walk with God.

Ancient and Medieval Swords:

The Word of God

Early swords were slender and made for thrusting. Later, they evolved to have broader blades suitable for both cutting and thrusting. To thrust is to impale, to strike a fatal blow. To cut is to notch, to carve, to cleave or separate.

This dual nature of the sword beautifully illustrates the power of God's Word. As Hebrews 4:12 (NIV) tells us: "For the word of God is alive and active. Sharper than any double-edged sword, it penetrates even to dividing soul and spirit, joints and marrow; it judges the thoughts and attitudes of the heart."

God's Word has the power to thrust deep into our hearts, exposing our innermost thoughts and motivations. It can also cut away the sinful and worldly influences in our lives, separating us unto God. This dual action of penetrating and dividing is what makes the Word so effective in our spiritual battles.

When we wield the Word of God, we're not just engaging in superficial combat. We're striking at the very root of sin and deception in our lives and in the world around us. The Word exposes what's hidden, bringing light to darkness and truth to lies. It separates truth from falsehood, holiness from sin, and God's ways from the world's ways.

The image of the sword is further emphasized in Revelation 1:16 (NLT):

"He held seven stars in his right hand, and a sharp two-edged sword came from his mouth. And his face was like the sun in all its brilliance."

This vivid description of Christ wielding the sword of His word reminds us of the authority and power behind the weapon we carry. When we speak God's Word, we're not speaking our own words, but the very words of Christ. This gives our spiritual sword an authority and power that no earthly weapon can match.

The Saber: Your Testimony

While the Word of God is our primary sword, we have another powerful weapon in our arsenal: our testimony. Like a saber, which has a large hand guard to protect the wielder's knuckles and fingers, our testimony shields us as we engage in spiritual warfare.

Revelation 12:11 (NLT) affirms this: "And they have defeated him by the blood of the Lamb and by their testimony. And they did not love their lives so much that they were afraid to die."

Our Testimony - the story of how God has worked in our lives - is a potent weapon against the enemy. It's a personal, sharp-edged tool that the enemy cannot refute or deny. When we share our testimony, we're not just telling a story; we're declaring the faithfulness and power of God in our lives.

Think about it: your testimony is unique to you. It's the story of how God has rescued you, transformed you, and used you for His glory. When you share your testimony, you're not just talking about abstract truths; you're providing living proof of God's power to change lives. This is why the enemy fears our testimonies so much - they provide irrefutable evidence of God's love and power.

Moreover, our testimonies serve as encouragement to others who are still in the midst of their battles. When we share how God has brought us through our trials, we give hope to those who are still struggling. Our stories become a lifeline for others, showing them that victory is possible through Christ.

Designing Your Sword

Just as each physical sword is unique, so too is each believer's spiritual sword. God has crafted you with intention and purpose, as Psalm 139:13-14 (The Voice) beautifully expresses:

"For You shaped me, inside and out. You knitted me together in my mother's womb long before I took my first breath. I will offer You my grateful heart, for I am Your unique creation, filled with wonder and awe. You have approached even the smallest details with excellence; Your works are wonderful; I carry this knowledge deep within my soul."

Your sword - your unique combination of God's Word and your personal testimony - is designed specifically for you and the battles you will face. No two swords are exactly alike because no two believers are exactly alike. God has uniquely gifted and called each of us, and our spiritual weapons reflect this individuality.

This customization extends to how we use God's Word. While the Bible is the same for all believers, how we apply it and which verses resonate most deeply with us can vary. Some may find their strength in the Psalms, others in the Epistles, and still others in the Gospels. This personalization of Scripture makes our spiritual sword even more effective, as we learn to wield it in a way that aligns with our unique calling and personality.

The Forging Process

Every sword must go through a rigorous forging process, and our spiritual swords are no exception. This process involves several crucial steps, each of which has a parallel in our spiritual growth:

1. ***Prepare your tools and materials:*** As 2 Timothy 2:15 (AMP) instructs, "Study and do

your best to present yourself to God approved, a workman [tested by trial] who has no reason to be ashamed, accurately handling and skillfully teaching the word of truth." This preparation involves immersing ourselves in God's Word, studying it diligently, and allowing it to shape our minds and hearts.

2. ***Heat:*** *Isaiah 48:10 (NIV) reminds us,* "See, I have refined you, though not as silver; I have tested you in the furnace of affliction." God uses the heat of trials to shape and strengthen us. These difficult times, though painful, are essential for our growth and refinement.

3. ***Shape the materials:*** We are shaped in God's image, as Genesis 1:27 (The Voice) declares, "So God did just that. He created humanity in His image, created them male and female." As

we yield to God's shaping process, we become more like Christ, reflecting His character and nature.

4. **Flatten:** This involves being hammered on both sides to ensure evenness. Jeremiah 23:29 (AMP) says, "Is not my word like fire [that consumes all that cannot endure the test]?" says the Lord, "and like a hammer that breaks the [most stubborn] rock [in pieces]?" God's Word works to flatten our pride and self-reliance, making us fit for His use.

5. **Heat and Cool:** This process happens repeatedly, reminding us of Romans 8:28 (AMP): "And we know [with great confidence] that God [who is deeply concerned about us] causes all things to work together [as a plan] for good for those who

love God, to those who are called according to His plan and purpose." The alternating periods of trial and rest in our lives serve to strengthen our faith and character.

6. ***Sanding:*** The Word of God smooths our rough edges. Isaiah 26:7 (NIV) says, "The path of the righteous is level; you, the Upright One, make the way of the righteous smooth." As we apply God's Word to our lives, it smooths out our imperfections and makes us more effective in His service.

7. ***Strengthening and Sharpening:*** This involves being quenched in oil, a process that must be done quickly and carefully. Galatians 6:9 (NLT) encourages us, "So let's not get tired of doing what is good. At just the right time we will reap a harvest of blessing if we don't give

up." Our obedience and perseverance in following God's Word strengthen us and sharpen our spiritual discernment.

8. ***Reheating:*** After quenching, the sword is slowly reheated to relieve stress. Genesis 8:22 (NIV) reminds us of the cyclical nature of life and growth: "As long as the earth endures, seedtime and harvest, cold and heat, summer and winter, day and night will never cease." This process reminds us that growth in our spiritual lives is ongoing, with seasons of intensity followed by periods of consolidation and rest.

9. ***Creating the Hilt:*** The handle is tailored to fit your hand, ensuring balance, and preventing slipping. This reminds us that God has equipped us perfectly for our unique calling.

He gives us the exact tools and abilities we need to fulfill His purpose for our lives.

10. *Sharpening:* The final step involves careful sharpening with fine tools. Proverbs 27:17 (NIV) tells us, "As iron sharpens iron, so one person sharpens another." This reminds us of the importance of fellowship and accountability in our spiritual growth. We need others to help us stay sharp and effective in our spiritual warfare.

The Finished Product

After this extensive process, we emerge as finely crafted weapons in God's arsenal. 1 Peter 2:9 (ASV) declares our identity:

"But ye are an elect race, a royal priesthood, a holy nation, a people for God's own possession, that ye may show forth the excellences of him who called you out of darkness into his marvelous light."

We are called to be both warriors and priests, wielding our swords with skill and reverence. This dual identity is crucial to understand. As warriors, we're called to engage in spiritual battle, to stand firm against the enemy's schemes, and to advance God's kingdom. As priests, we're called to minister to God and to others, to offer spiritual sacrifices, and to represent God to the world.

This finished product - a sharp, well-crafted sword in the hands of a skilled warrior-priest - is a formidable force in the spiritual realm. When we fully embrace our identity and wield our spiritual weapons skillfully, we become effective agents of God's power and love in the world.

Conclusion: It's All or Nothing

As we conclude this exploration of our spiritual swords, we must recognize the gravity of our calling. It truly is all or nothing. We cannot afford to be lukewarm or half-hearted in our approach to spiritual warfare. We must fully commit to the process of being shaped, sharpened, and wielded by God. **Revelation 3:15-16 (NIV)** warns us about the danger of lukewarm faith: "I know your deeds, that you are neither cold nor hot. I wish you were either one or the other! So, because you are lukewarm—neither hot nor cold—I am about to spit you out of my mouth." This stark warning reminds us that partial commitment is not an option in God's kingdom. We're called to be all in, fully devoted to our Lord and His purposes.

How you have been processed will determine if you are real or counterfeit. I encourage you to allow the Lord to process you fully. Ask the Holy

Spirit to reveal areas within you that have not been properly forged, and surrender those areas to Him. This might involve painful refinement, but remember that God's goal is to make you into an effective instrument for His glory.

Remember, you are not just any sword. You are a finely crafted weapon in the hand of the Almighty, designed for specific battles and unique purposes. Embrace your identity, submit to the forging process, and prepare to be wielded mightily for God's glory.

In the words of the apostle Paul in Ephesians 6:17 (NIV), "Take the helmet of salvation and the sword of the Spirit, which is the word of God." It's time to take up your sword and engage in the battles before you. For in God's army, it's truly all or nothing.

As you go forth, wielding your spiritual sword with skill and confidence, remember these key points:

1. Your sword is unique, designed specifically for you by the Master Craftsman.
2. The forging process, though sometimes painful, is essential for your effectiveness.
3. Both God's Word and your testimony are powerful weapons against the enemy.
4. You are called to be both a warrior and a priest in God's kingdom.
5. Half-hearted commitment is not an option - it's all or nothing.

May you go forth in the power of the Holy Spirit, your sword sharp and ready, prepared to face whatever battles lie ahead. For we know that in all these things, we are more than conquerors through Him who loved us (Romans 8:37). Amen.

STRATEGY EIGHT

SHEROS & HEROS

Author: Lee A. Williams, III

Proclamation of Our Divine Heritage

On the final day of the She Visions Worldwide Conference, Pastor Lee, begins with the powerful message starting in (1st Peter 2:9-10 AMPC) and it reads, "But you are a chosen race, a royal priesthood, a dedicated nation, [God's] own [a]purchased, special people, that you may set forth the wonderful deeds *and* display the virtues and perfections of Him Who called you out of darkness into His marvelous light. Once you were not a people [at all], but now you are God's people; once you were unpitied, but now you are pitied *and* have received mercy."

This scripture not only serves as a reminder of our divine heritage but also as a call to action for each one of us. We are not merely attendees at a conference; we are members of a divine lineage, carefully selected and set apart by God Himself.

This identity is not a passive attribute we carry; it's an active commission that demands proclamation. We are chosen to step out of the shadows of our former selves and into the light of God's purpose. This light is not meant to be hidden but to be shared openly, proclaiming His excellencies across the nations.

Consider the magnitude of transformation that this passage suggests. Once, we were not a people; we were scattered, isolated, and undefined. Now, we stand united under His name—not just as any people, but as God's people, embraced by His mercy. This shift from non-entity to a defined, purpose-driven community underlines the radical transformation God enacts in our lives.

It's essential for us to grasp the weight of being a 'royal priesthood.' This term shows a responsibility towards spiritual ministry, where each of us is called to mediate between the secular and the sacred, bringing God's message to the forefront in everyday situations. As a 'holy nation,' we are set apart, meant to live by and uphold divine principles that contrast sharply with worldly standards.

By embracing this identity, we embody the change He has made from what we were to what we have become. This conference should not be a series of sessions attended, but a transformational experience that redefines who we are and propels us into a future filled with His light. In carrying this new identity, let us walk boldly, upheld by the mercy we have received, and fervently proclaim the life-changing power of His grace.

To fully grasp the significance of this divine heritage, let's delve deeper into what it means to be a "chosen race, a royal priesthood, a holy nation." These are not mere titles, but profound callings that shape our identity and purpose.

As a chosen race, we are hand-picked by God, not based on our merits, but on His sovereign grace. This echoes the story of Israel, whom God chose not because they were the mightiest or most numerous, but because of His love (Deuteronomy 7:7-8). This choice places a responsibility on us to live up to our calling, to be a light to the nations, just as Israel was meant to be.

The concept of a royal priesthood combines two powerful roles. As royalty, we are children of the King, heirs to His kingdom, called to rule and reign with Christ. As priests, we are intermediaries between God and the world, bringing the needs of the world before God and bringing God's presence into the world. This dual role empowers us to influence our surroundings with godly authority while serving with Christ-like humility.

Being a holy nation sets us apart from the world's systems and values. Holiness isn't about rigid rule-following, but about being set apart for God's purposes. It's a call to be different, to stand out in a world that often pushes for conformity. Our holiness should be evident in our choices, our relationships, our work ethic, and our treatment of others.

The Echoes of Heros

The parallels between superheroes and our calling as believers run even deeper. Consider the concept of the *"secret identity"* common in superhero legends. Many superheroes live ordinary lives, only revealing their true powers when needed. Similarly, as believers, we may appear ordinary to the world, but we carry within us the extraordinary power of the Holy Spirit.

Furthermore, many superhero stories involve a moment of ***"origin"*** – a pivotal event that transforms an ordinary person into a hero. For Spider-Man, it was a bite from a radioactive spider. For us, it's the transformative power of salvation, the moment we accept Christ and are born again. This spiritual rebirth is our origin story, the moment we receive our ***"superpowers"*** of faith, hope, and love.

The idea of a ***"nemesis"*** is also prevalent in superhero narratives. Each hero has an arch-enemy that challenges them and pushes them to their limits. In our spiritual lives, we too face an adversary – not of flesh and blood, but the spiritual forces of evil (Ephesians 6:12). Our battles against temptation, doubt, and fear are just as real and intense as any superhero's fight against a supervillain.

Superheroes often have mentors who guide them in using their powers. Batman had Alfred, Spider-Man had Uncle Ben, and the X-Men had Professor Xavier. In our faith journey, we have spiritual mentors, Pastors, and ultimately, the Holy Spirit as our guide. These mentors help us understand our spiritual gifts and how to use them effectively for God's kingdom.

By drawing these parallels, we can see our faith journey as an epic adventure, full of challenges, growth, and victory. We are called to be everyday heroes, bringing light into darkness, hope into despair, and love into hatred. Our mission field is wherever God has placed us – our homes, workplaces, schools, and communities.

Lucas: A Tale of Discovery

Let me tell you a story. "There's a boy named Lucas. Lucas grew up in a small home, humble village unaware of his true Heritage. Lucas was known for his kindness and his leadership among his peers yet he often felt like there was more, he often felt like something was missing. Can you identify with that? And one day while exploring his late grandmother's attic, Lucas stumbles upon an old dusty chest and inside he found a set of ancient documents and a beautifully crafted Royal signate ring bearing a seal of a long-forgotten Kingdom."

In this humble beginning, Lucas embodies the quintessential journey many of us face—feeling that persistent tug in our hearts, that whisper of 'more' that the mundane facets of life cannot fulfill. It's a universal sentiment, the innate desire for purpose beyond daily routines, seeking a significance that aligns with a higher calling. Lucas, much like each of us at some point in our lives, was marked by an unshakeable feeling of potential, destined for something far greater than his immediate environment suggested.

Lucas's transformative discovery in his grandmother's attic symbolizes a pivotal moment of awakening that many believers experience. Just as Lucas found physical artifacts that reshaped his understanding of his identity, we, too, encounter spiritual truths that radically alter our perception of who we are. The ancient documents and the royal signet ring Lucas found were not just family heirlooms; they were undeniable proofs of his noble lineage, calling him to embrace a heritage he had never imagined.

This story resonates deeply with the biblical narrative of Moses, who lived as an ordinary shepherd until his divine encounter at the burning bush. Moses, like Lucas, was called out from his routine existence to lead Israel out of bondage. The ring Lucas found, bearing the seal of a long-forgotten kingdom, is akin to the divine commission Moses received—a symbol of authority and a mandate for leadership.

For Lucas, this discovery was just the beginning. It marked his journey towards embracing his true identity and the responsibilities that came with it. No longer was he merely Lucas from the village; he was Lucas, a rightful heir to a kingdom, called to reclaim and restore his family's legacy. His story teaches us that our past does not define us, nor does our present. Instead, our identity is often hidden, waiting to be discovered through divine revelation. Once revealed, it compels us to step into our role within God's grand narrative, just as Lucas did.

Thus, Lucas's tale is not merely a story from the past; it is a mirror reflecting our own spiritual journey. Each of us has a 'royal signet ring' to find within our own lives—a unique calling and identity in Christ that awaits our discovery. As we uncover our divine heritage, let us move forward with the courage and determination to fulfill the destiny that has been written for our lives, embracing the royal lineage to which we have been called.

The Concept of Identity

Our identity in Christ is not something we create but something we embrace and live out. Just as animals are identified by their distinct sounds - cat's meow, dogs bark, cows moo - we too should be identifiable by the "sound" we make in this world. The Apostle Paul reminds us in 2 Corinthians 5:17 (NKJV), "Therefore, if anyone is in Christ, he is a new creation; old things have passed away; behold, all things have become new." This new creation has a distinct identity that should be evident to the world around us.

The church, as a collective body of believers, doesn't sound like the culture around it; it sounds like the holiness of God. We are called to be set apart, as 1 Peter 1:16 (NKJV) states, "Be holy, for I am holy." This holiness is not about perfection, but about alignment with God's character and purposes.

Our identity in Christ is not just a label; it's a living reality that should permeate every aspect of our lives. John the Baptist reminds us, in 1 John 3:1 (NKJV), "Behold what manner of love the Father has bestowed on us, that we should be called children of God!" This identity as God's children should shape our thoughts, actions, and interactions with the world around us.

Moreover, our identity in Christ is secure and unchanging, unlike the shifting identities the world offers. As Paul declares in Colossians 3:3 (NKJV), "For you died, and your life is hidden with Christ in God." This hidden life is our true identity, anchored in the unchanging nature of Christ Himself.

Danger of Shapeshifting

One of the greatest threats to our effectiveness in spiritual warfare is becoming "shapeshifting believers." These are individuals who change their identity from day to day, putting on different costumes to fit in or to be what they desire to be. But our armor doesn't change with the weather of our circumstances. We must remain consistent in who we are in Christ.

The Apostle Paul warns against this in Ephesians 4:14 (NKJV): "that we should no longer be children, tossed to and fro and carried about with every wind of doctrine, by the trickery of men, in the cunning craftiness of deceitful plotting." Instead, we are called to "speak the truth in love" and "grow up in all things into Him who is the head—Christ" (Ephesians 4:15, NKJV).

The temptation to shape-shift often comes from a desire to fit in or avoid persecution. However, Jesus warned us about this in John 15:19 (NKJV), "If you were of the world, the world would love its own. Yet because you are not of the world, but I chose you out of the world, therefore the world hates you." Our distinct identity may bring opposition, but it also brings the opportunity to shine as lights in the darkness.

Shape-shifting can also stem from a lack of understanding of our true identity. As we grow in our knowledge of who we are in Christ, we become more secure and less likely to conform to the patterns of this world. This growth process is described in 2 Peter 1:3-4 (NKJV), "His divine power has given to us all things that pertain to life and godliness, through the knowledge of Him who called us by glory and virtue, by which have been given to us exceedingly great and precious promises, that through these you may be partakers of the divine nature, having escaped the corruption that is in the world through lust."

Embracing Our Chosen Status

You are a part of a chosen generation. God claims you as His own. This chosen status infuses us with supernatural authority, power, and strength. It's our first line of defense against the enemy's attacks on our purpose. The prophet Isaiah declares in Isaiah 43:1 (NKJV), "But now, thus says the Lord, who created you, O Jacob, And He who formed you, O Israel: 'Fear not, for I have redeemed you; I have called you by your name; You are Mine.'"

This chosen status is not based on our own merits or abilities, but on God's sovereign choice and love for us. As Ephesians 1:4-5 (NKJV) states, "Just as He chose us in Him before the foundation of the world, that we should be holy and without blame before Him in love, having predestined us to adoption as sons by Jesus Christ to Himself, according to the good pleasure of His will."

This chosen status is not just for our benefit, but for the benefit of others. As Peter reminds us in 1 Peter 2:9 (NKJV), we are chosen "that you may proclaim the praises of Him who called you out of darkness into His marvelous light." Our chosen status equips us to be witnesses and ambassadors for Christ in this world.

Furthermore, our chosen status gives us access to all the spiritual blessings in Christ. Paul elaborates on this in Ephesians 1:3-4 (NKJV), "Blessed be the

God and Father of our Lord Jesus Christ, who has blessed us with every spiritual blessing in the heavenly places in Christ, just as He chose us in Him before the foundation of the world, that we should be holy and without blame before Him in love." These blessings are our spiritual inheritance, empowering us to live out our divine purpose.

The High Calling of Priestly Work

Being chosen comes with a purpose - we are chosen for high calling, for priestly work. As priests, we carry a crown of glory. This priestly calling isn't about titles; it's about doing the work of a priest - serving, encouraging, praying, prophesying. It's about using our "priestly hood" in every situation, whether we feel prepared or not.

In the Old Testament, priests were mediators between God and the people. In the New Testament we all share this priestly role. As 1 Peter 2:5 (NKJV) says, "you also, as living stones, are being built up a spiritual house, a holy priesthood, to offer up spiritual sacrifices acceptable to God through Jesus Christ."

This priestly work involves intercession, as we stand in the gap for others. It involves proclamation, as we declare God's truth to a world in need. And it involves living a life of holiness, as we represent Christ to those around us.

Our priestly work also involves offering spiritual sacrifices. As Paul exhorts in Romans 12:1 (NKJV), "I beseech you therefore, brethren, by the mercies of God, that you present your bodies a living sacrifice, holy, acceptable to God, which is your reasonable service." This living sacrifice involves dedicating every aspect of our lives to God's service.

Moreover, our priestly calling includes the ministry of reconciliation. Paul explains this in 2

Corinthians 5:18-20 (NKJV), "Now all things are of God, who has reconciled us to Himself through Jesus Christ, and has given us the ministry of reconciliation... Now then, we are ambassadors for Christ, as though God were pleading through us: we implore you on Christ's behalf, be reconciled to God." As priests, we have the privilege and responsibility of helping others reconcile with God.

The Invitation

We've been invited not just to the table, but to the scene. While others might be fighting over seats at the table, we're called to be on the scene, making an impact wherever we go. This invitation is unique to each of us. You might be an option to everyone else, but to God, you're the only option for your specific purpose.

Jesus extends this invitation in Matthew 11:28-30 (NKJV): "Come to Me, all you who labor and are heavy laden, and I will give you rest. Take My yoke upon you and learn from Me, for I am gentle and lowly in heart, and you will find rest for your souls. For My yoke is easy and My burden is light."

This invitation is not just to salvation, but to a partnership with Christ in His mission. We are invited to be co-laborers with God, as 1st Corinthians 3:9 (NKJV) states, "For we are God's fellow workers; you are God's field, you are God's building."

This invitation is not just to service, but to intimate relationship with God. Jesus extends this invitation in John 15:15 (NKJV), "No longer do I call you servants, for a servant does not know what his master is doing; but I have called you friends, for all things that I heard from My Father I have made known to you." We are invited into the inner circle of God's friendship and confidence.

Furthermore, this invitation is to participate in God's divine nature. Peter explains this incredible privilege in 2 Peter 1:4 (NKJV), "by which have been given to us exceedingly great and precious promises, that through these you may be partakers of the divine nature, having escaped the corruption that is in the world through lust." We are invited to share in God's very nature, becoming more like Him as we walk in obedience to His call.

The Call to New Levels

Our identity and invitation call us to continually move to new levels. God has put an anointed staircase in front of us, inviting us to go higher. The prophet Isaiah paints a beautiful picture of this upward journey in Isaiah 40:31 (NKJV): "But those who wait on the Lord shall renew their strength; They shall mount up with wings like eagles, They shall run and not be weary, They shall walk and not faint."

New levels often mean new accountability, which can be intimidating. But remember, we are more accountable to things that don't benefit us eternally than we are to He who is our eternal benefit. As Paul reminds us in Philippians 3:13-14 (NKJV), "Brethren, I do not count myself to have apprehended; but one thing I do, forgetting those things which are behind and reaching forward to those things which are ahead, I press toward the goal for the prize of the upward call of God in Christ Jesus."

These new levels often require us to step out in faith, leaving behind the familiar and comfortable. Abraham's call in Genesis 12:1 (NKJV) illustrates this: "Now the Lord had said to Abram: 'Get out of your country, from your family and from your father's house, to a land that I will show you.'" Like Abraham, we may be called to leave the familiar behind as we step into new levels of faith and purpose.

Furthermore, these new levels often come with new challenges and opposition. As Paul warns in Philippians 1:29 (NKJV), "For to you it has been granted on behalf of Christ, not only to believe in Him, but also to suffer for His sake." Yet, these challenges are opportunities for growth and for God's power to be displayed in our lives.

The Anointing That Breaks Yokes

As we step into these new levels, we carry with us a powerful anointing. Isaiah 10:27 (KJV) tells us that "the yoke shall be destroyed because of the anointing." This anointing gives us the power to cast out demons, heal diseases, and bring deliverance. It's an essential part of our spiritual armor.

Jesus himself declared in Luke 4:18-19 (NKJV), "The Spirit of the Lord is upon Me, because

He has anointed Me to preach the gospel to the poor; He has sent Me to heal the brokenhearted, to proclaim liberty to the captives and recovery of sight to the blind, to set at liberty those who are oppressed; To proclaim the acceptable year of the Lord."

As followers of Christ, we carry this same anointing. We are empowered to continue the ministry of Jesus, breaking yokes of bondage and setting captives free.

This anointing is not just for our personal benefit, but for the advancement of God's kingdom. In Acts 1:8 (NKJV), Jesus promises, "But you shall receive power when the Holy Spirit has come upon you; and you shall be witnesses to Me in Jerusalem, and in all Judea and Samaria, and to the end of the earth." This anointing empowers us to be effective witnesses for Christ, breaking yokes of bondage not just in our lives, but in the lives of those around us.

Moreover, this anointing is renewable and sustainable. As Paul encourages in Ephesians 5:18 (NKJV), "And do not be drunk with wine, in which is dissipation; but be filled with the Spirit." The Greek tense here implies a continuous action - we are to be constantly filled with the Spirit, maintaining and renewing our anointing through consistent communion with God.

The Urgency of Now

The world needs what's inside of you now. God didn't let you be born too early or too late. He placed you in this generation for a reason. Whatever God has placed in your heart, now is the time to step out in faith and do it. The enemy would love nothing more than for you to delay your purpose.

The Apostle Paul emphasizes this urgency in 2nd Corinthians 6:2 (NKJV): "Behold, now is the accepted time; behold, now is the day of salvation."

And in Ephesians 5:15-16 (NKJV), he admonishes, "See then that you walk circumspectly, not as fools but as wise, redeeming the time, because the days are evil."

This urgency is not just about personal action, but about participating in God's redemptive work in the world. Jesus emphasized this in John 9:4 (NKJV), saying, "I must work the works of Him who sent Me while it is day; the night is coming when no one can work." We have a limited time to make an eternal impact, and every moment counts. This urgency should fuel our evangelistic efforts. Paul expresses this urgency in

Romans 10:14-15 (NKJV), "How then shall they call on Him in whom they have not believed? And how shall they believe in Him of whom they have not heard? And how shall they hear without a preacher? And how shall they preach unless they are sent?" The urgency of now compels us to share the gospel while we still have the opportunity.

May you walk in the fullness of your identity as you put on the full armor of God. May you boldly accept the invitation to new levels of faith and purpose. And may your impact be felt for generations to come as you stand firm against the enemies of purpose.

As we embrace this journey, we can draw inspiration from the great cloud of witnesses that have gone before us (Hebrews 12:1). From Abraham's faith to Moses' leadership, from David's passion to Paul's zeal, the Bible is filled with examples of individuals who stepped into their God-given destiny. Their stories remind us that God uses ordinary people to accomplish extraordinary things.

As you step into your role as a Shero or Hero in God's kingdom, remember the words of Joshua 1:9

(NKJV), "Have I not commanded you? Be strong and of good courage; do not be afraid, nor be dismayed, for the Lord your God is with you wherever you go." Your identity is secure in Christ, your invitation is sure, and your impact is needed.

In conclusion, as modern-day Sheros, and Heroes, we are called to a grand adventure of faith. Our mission field is vast, our resources are divine, and our Captain is infallible. Let us step forward with confidence, knowing that He who began a good work in us will carry it on to completion (Philippians 1:6). May we live lives that echo through eternity, leaving a legacy of faith for generations to come. For we are not just characters in a story – we are co-authors with God, writing the next chapter of His redemptive narrative in the world.

If you would like to watch Pastor Lee Williams, III preaching the closing message for our Annual *She*

Visions Worldwide Conference, use the URL listed below.

Sheros & Heros on You Tube ***https://bit.ly/3LeYRSo***

MEET TAUNDRA D. WILLIAMS
"The Destiny Midwife"
AUTHOR & VISIONARY

Taundra D. Williams, also known as the Destiny Midwife, is the CEO and founder of Destiny Speaks International, LLC - a ministry devoted to helping individuals move from hurt to a healed and from trauma to freedom. Driven by her desire to see people saved, delivered, and set free, Taundra dedicates her life to praying for people wherever God leads her. Destiny Speaks was established after Taundra had a profound spiritual encounter with the Lord. Driven by purpose, Taundra vowed to do exactly what God instructed her to do. Taundra founded Destiny Speaks in order to create a secure and welcoming environment outside of the church walls where individuals could discover their identity in Christ. To document the transformative power of the Lord Jesus Christ, God instructed Taundra to gather the testimonies of the partners in her church since giving him their complete yes. This birthed a movement, which she then published their first work entitled Eyes Have Not Seen The Testimonies of Our Yes. With over 20 years of experience in the ministry, Taundra loving says we need Jesus and a therapist. Becoming educated about this human body and our spiritual side is very important to becoming completely whole. Taundra also holds an educational background in Business and Entrepreneurship, and she uses her preaching and teaching style to shatter the strongholds of rejection and past pain. She has dedicated her life to God and continues you increase her knowledge of the issues in the tissues, also known as TRAUMA.

Taundra is a certified Master Life & Transformation Coach, Speaker, Mentor, Author, and Book Publisher. Every book birthed from the process of evicting trauma, helps each individual become whole and free. This process of a complete YES to God birthed THE UNMUTED EVERYWHERE NATION! Becoming unmuted herself has helped her push others into purpose by providing a platform for others to share their stories through conference speaking and book writing. She is dedicated to going to the nations as she has been instructed. The very First Shatter The Glass Ceiling tour began in 2022 and there is no slowing down, She is preparing for future tours throughout the states and overseas. Dedicated to making sure each author is ready to share and their testimonies and the word of God she is working hard to reach different countries and overcome language barriers, believing that everything God revealed to her will come to past. Through prayer, fasting, and inner healing, She is committed to helping each person she encounters to live the life God has purposed for them. Taundra is married to her "purpose partner" Lee A Williams, III, a certified church planter and Pastor. Together they planted The Launch Church located in San Antonio, Texas where she serves as Lead Pastor alongside him. She is also a mother of four and grandmother to three grand girls.

Despite her busy schedule, Taundra spends time with her family, pushing individuals from mediocre living to a wholly life from the inside out. If you crave deeper understanding of your unique, God-breathed purpose and the confidence to powerfully pursue it, this manual is for you. No more wavering, no more defeat - you were born for such a time as this. You can find The Destiny Midwife on social media platforms.

Facebook: Taundra D. Williams

Instagram & TikTok: destiny_midwife

Website: www.destinyspeaks.org

If you are interested in publishing your testimony/story and traveling with other like-minded individuals, please visit www.destinyspeaks.org for more information.

MEET DR. MICHELLE ROUCHE

Michelle can best be described as a cheerleader for all women. She uses her platform to champion for women through conferences, workshops, her digital publication, and group coaching. Michelle's passion for creating change is obvious to those all around her. Her winning attitude and stand-out personality command a response. She is a natural-born entrepreneur with her first business being a newspaper girl at the age of 12. She is a Marketing Executive by training, an author, sought after Keynote speaker, Founder of She Is International, Editor-in-chief of She Is Magazine, a Certified Transformation Coach, an Ambassador for Brown Skin Brunchin;' an international social group, founded in 2018 around a simple idea - brunch and a CASA Advocate. She's Brian's wife, a cool mom (I wasn't always) and a Lolli (my alternate name for grandma-- Brian and I are Lolli & Pop Pop) to Avery and Arlo and Ace. She is also an established Realtor and a trusted real estate advisor specializing in assisting first-time buyers.

Michelle and her family currently reside in San Antonio, Texas however she has deep roots in her hometown of Savannah, Georgia. She is an alumni of Savannah State University where she earned her Bachelors of Business. Michelle also holds an honorary doctorate from San Antonio Theological College. She has used her platform and influence to empower and shift women of all ages; giving them permission to think differently and DREAM AGAIN. Her message centers on mindset shifting. "If you can think a new thought you can build a new dream". If you listen intently; her message will cause you to change or be challenged, consequently it is impossible to remain the same after an encounter. Michelle believes that there is a seed inside of every woman. Her mantra is, —Find a woman and water her.

You can find Dr. Rouche on all social media platforms **@michellrouche.**

MEET PASTOR LAURA E. TORRES

Pastor Laura E. Torres, a devoted wife of 31 years and loving mother to 8, proudly embraces the role of Grammie to 9 princesses and 1 prince. With a diverse career spanning various domains, she embodies leadership and mentorship.

As a Pastor, Mentor, Realtor, Motivational Speaker, Author, her influence extends far beyond the pulpit. Since 2009, alongside her husband, she's co-founded transformative Men & Women's Campuses in San Antonio, bringing change to countless lives.

Grounded in unwavering faith, Pastor Laura lives by mottos like "Reaching the Lost at any cost," guiding her actions and inspiring others. Immersed in ministry since age 20, she's driven by a profound calling to serve, guided by favorite scriptures Isaiah 61:1-4 and Isaiah 43:18-19.

Her commitment to positive change extends to her writing, with her first book set to release soon.

Beyond her professional endeavors, she finds joy in culinary pursuits, hosting gatherings, and mentoring at her kitchen table. Her love for travel and commitment to mentorship are evident as she embraces moments spent with her family and spiritual community, leaving an indelible mark on all whose lives she touches. You can find Pastor Laura on Facebook @lauratorres

MEET PROPHET APRYL ESSIEN

Prophet Essien is a Native of Beaumont, TX. She currently resides in San Antonio, TX where she is the happily, SUBMITTED wife of Deacon Kevin Essien. Together they are stewards over the lives of 3 beautiful children--Ahli, Khingston and A'Zelliyah! Prophet Apryl has been committed to the call and cause of Christ for more than 20 years.

She was Saved and filled with Holy Spirit and gifted with the evidence of tongues at the age of 15. She answered the call to the Prophetic Office at the age of 18 and has been preaching the unadulterated Gospel ever since! While her mantle is drenched with transparency and deliverance, it is equally soaked in compassion and humility.

Her heart belongs to God and to His people. Her earnest desire is to please the Father and serve with clean hands and a pure heart. This is why she's a

State Certified Christian Chaplain and Christian Counselor. Her mission and goal in life is to be about The Kingdom and reconciling the lost souls back to The Father.

MEET CAROL M. HARDY

Carol Hardy is the founder of "Unapologetic Women's Ministry" and ministers alongside her husband Lamond in "The Power of Three Marriage Ministry." Together, they have ministered to many. Carol is the mother of four amazing children and has a grandson she adores. She works a full-time job while doing ministry and assisting her husband with multiple aspects of their business. Carol and Lamond attend The Rock San Antonio, where they are under the care of Apostle Kevin Duhart and Lisa Duhart.

Carol has a heart for God and God's people, and the focal point of her ministry is to cultivate women by encouraging them and building them up in their identity in Christ. Carol believes that when we know our identity, we live an unapologetic life for Christ. When we live an unapologetic life for Christ, we can teach and empower others to do the same.

She also believes that teaching the word of God is imperative to a believer's foundation. She is Holy Spirit-led and stands for the gospel of Jesus Christ. You can find Carol on all social media platforms **@carolhardy and @unapolog3tic.**

MEET PASTOR LEE WILLIAMS, III

L.A. Williams, III *"The Purpose Pointer"*, born October 16, 1981, in Houston, Texas, Senior Pastor L. A. Williams, Jr. and Vanessa Williams. He is a passionate preacher, teacher, and author dedicated to helping individuals discover their true identity in Christ and fulfill their God-given purpose.

With over 25 years in the ministry, he answered his call to ministry in 1999 and delivered his first sermon at Wheatley Heights Baptist Church in San Antonio, Texas. As the Founding Pastor of The Launch Church and a Church Strategist for Central and East Texas through the Baptist General Convention of Texas, he has served in various pastoral roles including Youth Pastor, Assistant Pastor, and Senior Pastor. He has successfully planted, merged, and revitalized churches since 2008.

He's the visionary behind the Methods Conference and Cohorts, which equips ministry and marketplace leaders through workshops and development programs. His consulting work spans Texas and the NW Pacific region, helping transform small congregations into strategically impactful communities.

L.A. Williams, III, resides in San Antonio, TX with his wife Taundra D. Williams ("The Destiny Midwife"), and has four grown children, three granddaughters, and extended family. He maintains active involvement in various community and religious organizations, including the Guadalupe District Association Inc. & Baptist Ministers Union.

He believes every learner, with God and clear goals, can grow into a life-changing leader.

With multiple certifications, licenses, and skills he has become an entrepreneur and small business owner. L.A. Williams, III is the visionary behind the Methods Conference and Cohorts, equipping ministry, and marketplace leaders to develop generational leadership through workshops, development programs, and strategic resources. His consulting work spans Texas and the NW Pacific region, revitalizing churches and helping them experience both spiritual and organizational growth.

L.A. Williams, III's influence extends through various conferences, networks, and partnerships, connecting him to broader movements and resources that fuel his strategic leadership. His mission is to empower leaders and churches to fulfill their potential, advancing the Kingdom of God through transformational leadership.

L.A. Williams, III continues to pursue his calling to inspire and empower believers to make a lasting impact in their generation to fulfill their purpose!

You can Find The — Purpose Pointer on social media platforms below.

Facebook: https://www.facebook.com/preachla

Instagram: lawilliamsx3

www.ingramcontent.com/pod-product-compliance
Lightning Source LLC
Chambersburg PA
CBHW070645160426
43194CB00009B/1585